THE CALIFORNIA DIRECTORY OF
FINE WINERIES

FIFTH EDITION

THE CALIFORNIA DIRECTORY OF
FineWineries

K. Reka Badger and Marty Olmstead, Writers

Robert Holmes, Photographer

Tom Silberkleit, Editor and Publisher

WINE HOUSE PRESS

CONTENTS

INTRODUCTION

Whether you are a visitor or a native seeking the ultimate chalice of nectar from the grape, navigating Northern California's wine country can be intimidating. Hundreds of wineries—from glamorous estates to converted barns, from nationally recognized labels to hidden gems—are found throughout Napa, Sonoma, and Mendocino. The challenge is deciding where to go and how to plan a trip. This book will be your indispensable traveling companion.

The sixty-eight wineries in this fully updated, fifth edition of *The California Directory of Fine Wineries* are known for producing some of the world's most admired wines. From the moment you walk in the door of these wineries, you will be greeted like a guest and invited to sample at a relaxing, leisurely tempo. Although the quality of the winemaker's art is of paramount importance, the wineries are also notable as tourist destinations. Many boast award-winning contemporary architecture, while others are housed in lovingly preserved historical structures. Some have galleries featuring museum-quality artwork by local and international artists or exhibits focusing on the region's past and the history of winemaking. You will also enjoy taking informative behind-the-scenes tours, exploring inspirational gardens, and participating in celebrated culinary programs. With a bit of advance planning, you can arrange to take part in a barrel sampling, a blending seminar, or a grape stomping.

As you explore this magnificent region, you'll encounter some of California's most appealing scenery and attractions—mountain ranges, rugged coastline, pastures with majestic oak trees, abundant parkland, renowned spas, and historic towns. Use the information in this book to plan your trip, and be sure to stop along the way and take in the sights. You have my promise that traveling to your destination will be as pleasurable as the wine tasted upon your welcome.

—Tom Silberkleit
Editor and Publisher
Wine House Press
Sonoma, California

THE ETIQUETTE OF WINE TASTING

Most of the wineries profiled in this book offer amenities ranging from lush gardens to art exhibitions, but their main attraction is the tasting room. This is where winery employees get a chance to share their products and knowledge with consumers, in hopes of establishing a lifelong relationship. They are there to please.

Yet, for some visitors, the ritual of tasting fine wines can be intimidating. Perhaps it's because swirling wine and using a spit bucket seem to be unnatural acts. But with a few tips, even a first-time taster can enjoy the experience. After all, the point of tasting is to enhance your knowledge by learning the differences among varieties of wines, styles of winemaking, and appellations.

A list of available wines is usually posted, beginning with whites and ending with the heaviest reds or, if available, dessert wines. Look for the tasting notes, which are typically set out on the counter; refer to them as you taste each wine. A number of wineries charge a tasting fee for three or four wines of your choosing or for a "flight"—most often three preselected wines. In any event, the tasting process is the same.

After you are served, hold the stem of the glass with your thumb and as many fingers as you need to maintain control. Lift the glass up to the light and note the color and intensity of the wine. Good wines tend to be bright, with the color fading near the rim. Next, gently swirl the wine in the glass. Observe how much of the wine adheres to the sides of the glass. If lines—called legs—are visible, the wine is viscous, indicating body or weight as well as a high alcohol content. Now, tip the glass to about a 45-degree angle, take a short sniff, and concentrate on the aromas. Swirl the wine again to aerate it, releasing additional aromas. Take another sniff and see if the "bouquet" reminds you of anything—rose petals, citrus fruit, or a freshly ironed pillowcase, for example—that will help you identify the aroma.

Finally, take a sip and swirl the wine around your tongue, letting your taste buds pick up all the flavors. The wine may remind you of honey or cherries or mint—as with the "nosing," try to make as many associations as you can. Then spit the wine into the bucket on the counter. Afterward, notice how long the flavor stays in your mouth; a long finish is the ideal. If you don't want another taste, just pour the wine remaining in your glass into the bucket and move on. Remember, the more you spit or pour out, the more wines you can sample.

The next level of wine tasting involves guided tastings and food-and-wine pairings. In these sessions, a few cheeses or a series of appetizers are paired with a flight of wines, usually a selection of three red or three white wines presented in the recommended order of tasting. The server will explain what goes with what.

If you still feel self-conscious, practice at home. Once you are in a real tasting room, you'll be better able to focus on the wine itself. That's the real payoff, because once you learn what you like and why you like it, you'll be able to recognize wines in a similar vein anywhere in the world.

What Is an Appellation?

The word *appellation* is often used to refer to the geographical area where wine grapes were grown. If the appellation is named on the bottle label, it means that at least 85 percent of the wine is from that area.

The terms "appellation of origin" and "American Viticultural Area" (AVA) are frequently used interchangeably in casual conversation, but they are not synonymous. In the United States, appellations follow geopolitical borders, such as state and county lines, rather than geographic boundaries. AVAs are defined by such natural features as soil types, climate, and topography.

The U.S. Alcohol and Tobacco Tax and Trade Bureau is the arbiter of what does and does not qualify as an AVA. A winery or other interested party that wants a particular area to qualify as an official AVA must supply proof that it has enough specific attributes to distinguish it significantly from its neighbors.

Why do winemakers care? Because it is far more prestigious—and informative—to label a wine with an appellation such as Sonoma County, Napa Valley, or Russian River Valley than with the more generic California, which means the grapes could have come from the Central Valley or anywhere else in the state. Moreover, informed consumers learn that a Chardonnay from the Alexander Valley, for instance, is apt to smell and taste different from one originating in the Russian River Valley. A winery may be located in one appellation but use grapes from another to make a particular wine. In this case, the appellation on the label would indicate the source of the grapes rather than the physical location of the winery.

The following are the appellations in Napa, Sonoma, and Mendocino:

NAPA

Atlas Peak

Calistoga

Chiles Valley District

Diamond Mountain District

Howell Mountain

Los Carneros

Mount Veeder

Napa Valley

Oak Knoll District

Oakville

Rutherford

Spring Mountain District

St. Helena

Stags Leap District

Wild Horse Valley

Yountville

SONOMA

Alexander Valley

Bennett Valley

Chalk Hill

Dry Creek Valley

Green Valley

Knight's Valley

Los Carneros

North Coast

Northern Sonoma

Rockpile

Russian River Valley

Sonoma Coast

Sonoma Mountain

Sonoma Valley

MENDOCINO

Anderson Valley

Cole Ranch

Covelo

Dos Rios

McDowell Valley

Mendocino

Mendocino Ridge

Potter Valley

Redwood Valley

Sanel Valley (pending)

Ukiah Valley (pending)

Yorkville Highlands

NAPA

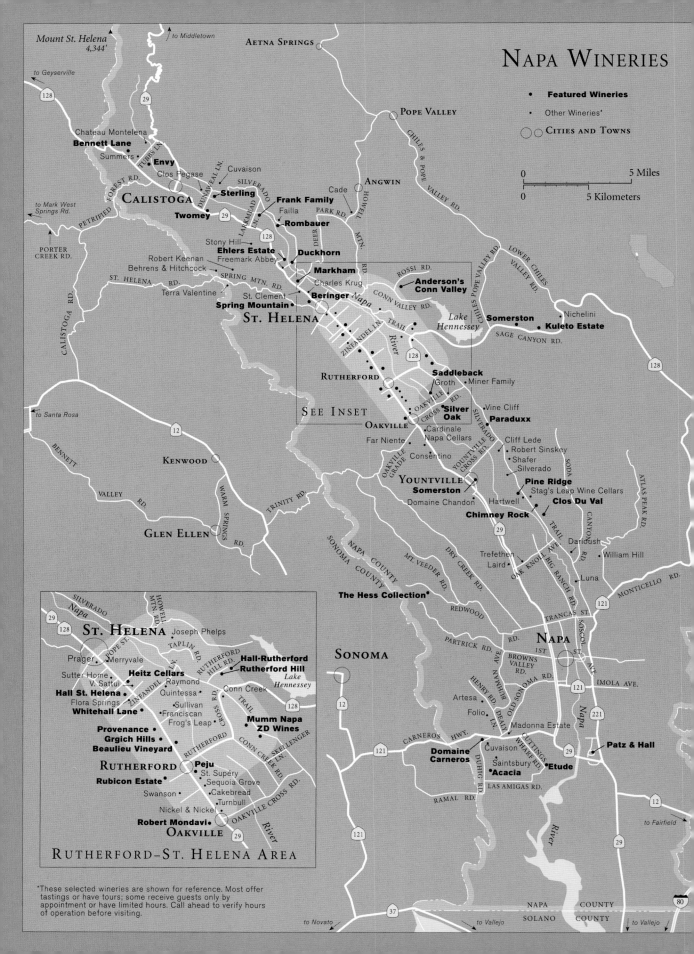

The Napa Valley, jam-packed with hundreds of premium wineries and thousands of acres of coveted vineyards, has earned its position as the country's number one winemaking region. From its southern tip at San Pablo Bay, about an hour's drive from San Francisco, this picture-perfect patchwork of agriculture extends thirty miles north to the dramatic Palisades that tower above Calistoga. The narrow, scenic valley is defined on the east by a series of hills known as the Vaca Range and on the west by the rugged peaks of the Mayacamas Range, including the steep forested slopes of Mount Veeder. St. Helena, where upscale stores and chic boutiques line the historic Main Street, is the jewel in the region's crown. At the southern end of the valley, the city of Napa has experienced a boom in recent years, with a plethora of restaurants and attractions such as the vibrant Oxbow Public Market. The mostly two-lane Highway 29 links these and smaller towns that welcome visitors with a variety of spas, restaurants, and bed-and-breakfast inns.

For an unforgettable impression, book a hot-air balloon ride or simply drive up the winding Oakville Grade and pull over at the top for a view worthy of a magazine cover.

ACACIA VINEYARD

Acacia Vineyard ranks among the Pinot Noir pioneers of the Carneros appellation, a region of farmland and tidal marshes stretching north from San Pablo Bay. Due to the proximity of the bay, the winery basks in a maritime climate of morning fog and ocean breezes. Air temperatures average ten degrees cooler than those in upper Napa Valley, making Carneros perfect for growing the winery's specialties: Pinot Noir and Chardonnay.

Founded in 1979, the winery initially bought fruit from St. Clair Vineyard, a neighbor across the street. With its inaugural harvest, Acacia Vineyard became one of the first in California to produce a single-vineyard Pinot Noir. The winery continues to craft Pinot Noir from the old Martini clones growing in the dry-farmed St. Clair Vineyard, a vinicultural legacy that represents one of the nation's longest runs of consecutive bottlings of wine pur-

chased from a single vineyard. Lone Tree Vineyard—named for an ancient acacia growing among the vines—is an estate planting that boasts thirteen different Pinot Noir clones. The winery's Chardonnay comes from both estate and purchased fruit grown in Carneros, with several single-vineyard offerings sourced from the Russian River Valley appellation.

An important stop along the Pacific Flyway, the Carneros region hosts many birds, including more than two dozen species of waterfowl, as well as egrets, western bluebirds, and red-tailed hawks. It is also home to threatened or endangered species. To help support them, Acacia makes a special wine, Marsh Chardonnay, sold exclusively at the winery, and donates proceeds from sales of the wine to a fund dedicated to the restoration and ongoing care of local wetlands.

An elongated complex of cocoa-brown buildings, Acacia Vineyard is a working winery with the crush pad located in front. Tucked beside the cellar, the boutique-style tasting room features a rustic chandelier and furnishings that convey a farm-to-table feeling. Glass doors open into one of the massive white barrel rooms containing hundreds of American and French and other European oak barrels.

On weekends, tastings frequently take place in the cellar, among stainless steel tanks emitting the fruity aroma of wine in various stages of development. As visitors gather around the long wood tasting bar, the scene evokes the intimate wine country experience of thirty years ago. On clear days, visitors stepping out the front door of the tasting room can see San Pablo Bay glittering in the distance, as well as 2,571-foot Mount Tamalpais to the southwest, 3,848-foot Mount Diablo to the southeast, and buildings rising from the heart of San Francisco fifty miles away.

ACACIA VINEYARD
2750 Las Amigas Rd.
Napa, CA 94558
707-226-9991, ext. 2
877-266-1700, ext. 2
acacia.info@
acaciavineyard.com
www.acaciavineyard.com

OWNER: Diageo Chateau and Estate Wines.

LOCATION: About 5 miles southwest of the town of Napa.

APPELLATION: Los Carneros.

HOURS: 10 A.M.–4 P.M. Monday–Saturday; noon–4 P.M. Sunday.

TASTINGS: $15 for 5 or 6 wines. Reservations required.

TOURS: By appointment.

THE WINES: Chardonnay, Pinot Noir, Syrah, Viognier.

SPECIALTIES: Single-vineyard Chardonnay and Pinot Noir.

WINEMAKER: Matthew Glynn.

ANNUAL PRODUCTION: 90,000 cases.

OF SPECIAL NOTE: Most single-vineyard wines available in tasting room only.

NEARBY ATTRACTIONS: di Rosa Preserve (indoor and outdoor exhibits of works by contemporary Bay Area artists); Napa Valley Opera House.

ANDERSON'S CONN VALLEY VINEYARDS

ANDERSON'S CONN VALLEY VINEYARDS
680 Rossi Rd.
St. Helena, CA 94574
707-963-8600
800-946-3497
info@connvalleyvineyards.com
www.connvalleyvineyards.com

OWNERS: Anderson family.

LOCATION: 3.3 miles east of Silverado Trail via Howell Mountain Rd. and Conn Valley Rd.

APPELLATION: Napa Valley.

HOURS: 10 A.M.–4 P.M. Monday–Friday; 10 A.M.–2 P.M. Saturday.

TASTINGS: By appointment. Complimentary for current release wines.

TOURS: By appointment. 10 A.M., 12 P.M., 2 P.M., and 4 P.M., Monday–Friday; 10 A.M., 12 P.M., and 2 P.M., Saturday.

THE WINES: Cabernet Sauvignon, Chardonnay, Pinot Noir, Sauvignon Blanc.

SPECIALTIES: Cabernet Sauvignon, Bordeaux blends.

WINEMAKER: Mac Sawyer.

ANNUAL PRODUCTION: 8,500 cases.

OF SPECIAL NOTE: Barrel tasting, lunch, and other special events are available at varying prices by advance arrangement. Tours and tastings are held in extensive winery caves.

NEARBY ATTRACTIONS: Bothe-Napa State Park (hiking, picnicking, horseback riding, swimming Memorial Day–Labor Day); Silverado Museum (Robert Louis Stevenson memorabilia).

Less than a ten-minute drive from bustling downtown St. Helena, Anderson's Conn Valley Vineyards occupies a niche in a valley within a valley. The location is so remote that most drivers along Conn Valley Road aren't even aware the winery exists. Out here, you could hear a pin drop, except during the busy harvest season that begins in late summer.

Anderson's Conn Valley Vineyards was founded in 1983 by Gus and Todd Anderson along with their wives, Phyllis and Dana. Gus Anderson spearheaded the lengthy search for vineyard property in Napa Valley. He had the advantage of realizing Napa's tremendous potential before the region became widely known (in the wake of the famous 1976 Paris tasting that put Napa on the world wine map) and before land in wine country became prohibitively expensive.

Joseph Heitz and Joseph Phelps had already established wineries in the neighborhood by the time the Andersons found their dream site, forty acres in the eastern part of the St. Helena American Viticultural Area near the base of Howell Mountain. Unfortunately, the acreage was not for sale; it would take fifteen months of negotiations to secure the property.

Then the real work of establishing a winery operation began, and for the most part, it has all been done by the Andersons. Todd Anderson left his profession as a geophysicist to pound posts, hammer nails, and install twenty-six and a half acres of prime vineyards. That was just the beginning. While the vines matured, the Andersons created a fifteen-acre-foot reservoir and built the winery, the residence, and a modest cave system.

The family did hire professionals with the necessary heavy-duty equipment to expand the caves by eight thousand square feet. Completed in 2001, the nine-thousand-square-foot caves feature a warren of narrow pathways beneath the hillside. Deep in the caverns, one wall has been pushed out to make way for tables and chairs where visitors can sample the wines. In clement weather, tastings are often held on the far side of the caves, with seating beneath market umbrellas at tables that overlook the reservoir.

Tours and tastings are led by Todd Anderson or his wife, Ronene, who now operate Anderson's Conn Valley Vineyards. A great advantage to touring a family winery is the chance to get to know the people behind the wines and to linger long enough to ask questions that might never get answered during a large group tour at one of Napa's big and better-known wineries located along either Highway 29 or the Silverado Trail.

BEAULIEU VINEYARD

BEAULIEU VINEYARD
1960 St. Helena Hwy.
Rutherford, CA 94573
800-264-6918, ext. 5233
707-967-5233
visitingbv@bvwines.com
www.bvwines.com

OWNER: Diageo Chateau
and Estate Wines.

LOCATION: About 3 miles
south of St. Helena.

APPELLATION: Rutherford.

HOURS: 10 A.M.–5 P.M. daily.

TASTINGS: Maestro White
Wine Tasting, $15 for choice
of 4 wines from winery-only
Maestro series. Cabernet
Tasting, $20 for vineyard and
clonal selections exclusive to
BV. Reserve Tasting, $30 for
current and library Georges
de Latour Private Reserve
Cabernet Sauvignon. Retro-
spective Reserve Tasting,
$50 for a flight of 4 Georges
de Latour Private Reserve
Cabernet Sauvignon;
reservations required.

TOURS: Historic Tour and
Barrel Tasting ($40) includes
tour of the 1885 winery and
BV museum; reservations
required.

THE WINES: Cabernet Sauvignon, Chardonnay, Merlot,
Sauvignon Blanc.

SPECIALTIES: Rutherford
Cabernet Sauvignon,
Georges de Latour Private
Reserve Cabernet Sauvignon.

WINEMAKER: Jeffrey Stambor.

ANNUAL PRODUCTION:
300,000 cases.

OF SPECIAL NOTE: 15 small-lot
wines available in tasting
room only. Clone series
(Cabernet Sauvignon) and
Reserve Tapestry series
(Bordeaux blends) available
in the Reserve Room.

NEARBY ATTRACTION:
Culinary Institute of America
at Greystone (cooking
demonstrations).

French immigrant and cream of tartar magnate Georges de Latour and his wife, Fernande, bought their first Rutherford ranch in 1900. "Beau lieu!" Fernande declared when she saw the ranch, deeming it a "beautiful place." Thus, Beaulieu Vineyard, also known simply as BV, was named. Among the first to recognize Rutherford's potential for yielding stellar Cabernet Sauvignon, Georges de Latour was determined to craft wine to rival the French. By 1909 he had expanded his vineyard and established a nursery for cultivating phylloxera-resistant rootstock. For a time, the nursery supplied a half-million grafted vines annually to California vineyards.

In 1938 de Latour hired André Tchelistcheff, who declared Sauvignon worthy of flagship he introduced a number of including controlling heat during and protect delicate fruit flavors, than American, oak barrels for components. As a result, BV's Private Reserve became Napa Valley's first "cult Cab" and continues to rank among the region's most widely collected wines.

fabled, Russian-born enologist the 1936 Private Reserve Cabernet status. With de Latour's blessing, practices now considered standard, fermentation to keep wines cool and barrel aging in French, rather the addition of more nuanced

Housed in a Boston ivy–clad complex built in three different centuries, the gray stone and concrete winery faces the visitor center across a parking lot studded with sycamores and oaks. Guests follow a path edged with manicured boxwood and roses to reach the center, a two-story, hexagonal building with stone exterior. Upon entering, they are immediately handed a complimentary glass of wine in homage to Mrs. de Latour's peerless hospitality. Natural light spills from above, bathing the redwood interior. A curved staircase leads down an open well to the Club Room, where visitors who reserve ahead can enjoy a seated tasting.

A few steps from the visitor center is the Reserve Room, dedicated to the winery's flagship Georges de Latour Private Reserve Cabernet Sauvignon. At a softly lit marble-topped bar, visitors can taste winery exclusives and library wines, or purchase vintages of the Private Reserve going back to 1970. Fieldstone walls mimic those of BV's core winery, built in 1885. In a cozy side room, a glass-topped table displays bottles representing singular moments in the winery's history, includ-ing a release of Pure Altar Wine vinified during Prohibition. A brilliant businessman, de Latour prospered despite grape shortages, insect infestations, and Prohibition. More than a century later, Beaulieu Vineyard reigns as a leader in the production of acclaimed Cabernet Sauvignon and the longest continually operated winery in Napa Valley.

BENNETT LANE WINERY

BENNETT LANE WINERY
3340 Hwy. 128
Calistoga, CA 94515
877-629-6272
info@bennettlane.com
www.bennettlane.com

OWNERS: Randy and
Lisa Lynch.

LOCATION: About 2 miles
north of Calistoga.

APPELLATION: Napa Valley.

HOURS: 10 A.M.–5:30 P.M.
daily.

TASTINGS: $10 for 4 wines.

TOURS: Daily, by
appointment.

THE WINES: Cabernet
Sauvignon, Chardonnay,
Maximus (a red blend),
Port, White Maximus
(a white blend).

SPECIALTIES: Cabernet
Sauvignon, Maximus.

WINEMAKER: Grant
Hermann.

ANNUAL PRODUCTION:
12,000 cases.

OF SPECIAL NOTE: Blending
experiences for groups
of 6 or more ($175
per person). Reserve
Chardonnay and Syrah
available only at tasting
room. Annual events
include Cabernet Release
Weekend (February).

NEARBY ATTRACTIONS:
Old Faithful Geyser of
California; Robert Louis
Stevenson State Park
(hiking).

Far from the din and traffic of central Napa Valley, Bennett Lane Winery lures the adventuresome Cabernet lover to the northernmost wedge of the valley, where the Vaca Range meets the Mayacamas Range. This sequestered setting just north of the town of Calistoga features dramatic views of Mount St. Helena and the Palisades as well as a manicured lawn for picnicking in peace. It is an ideal backdrop for Bennett Lane's hand-crafted, small-production wines. At the front end of the Mediterranean-style winery, a small, sparsely decorated tasting room fits the low-key ambience of the surroundings.

Owners Randy and Lisa  Lynch were relative newcomers to the world of wine in 2003 when they purchased what had once been a custom crush facility. Originally, they had been looking for a second home with vineyard land, and soon after purchasing a residence in Calistoga, they bought the Bennett Lane property. The Lynches were encouraged by critical praise for their wines, whose fruit now comes from highly acclaimed sources in Napa Valley. These vineyards are dotted throughout the valley, from Yountville in the south to Randy Lynch's vineyard in Calistoga in the north. Lynch's goal is to create wines that are both approachable and complex, what he calls "the best of both worlds, meaning you can drink them today, but they are structured enough to cellar for several years."

Bennett Lane's signature wine is named Maximus, after the second-century Roman emperor Magnus Maximus, a noted vinophile of his day. The exact percentages of varietals that go into the Maximus wines vary somewhat from vintage to vintage. The 2006 Maximus Red Feasting Wine is a typical blend, with 64 percent Cabernet Sauvignon, 19 percent Merlot, 9 percent Syrah, 5 percent Malbec, and 3 percent Petit Verdot. At Bennett Lane, blending is the name of the game. The winery offers a custom blending experience, called Put a Cork in It, for groups of six to eight guests who participate in a blending session. Each receives a blended bottle of wine.

BERINGER VINEYARDS

With the 1883 Rhine House, hand-carved aging tunnels, and a heritage dating to 1876, Beringer Vineyards is steeped in history like few other wineries in California. The oldest continuously operating winery in Napa Valley, it combines age-old traditions with up-to-date technology to create a wide range of award-winning wines.

It was German know-how that set the Beringer brothers on the path to glory. Jacob and Frederick Beringer emigrated from Mainz, Germany, to the United States in the 1860s. Jacob, having worked in cellars in  Germany, was intrigued when he heard that the California climate was ideal for growing the varietal grapes that flourished in Europe's winemaking regions. Leaving Frederick in New York, he traveled west in 1870 to discover that Napa Valley's rocky, well-drained soils were similar to those in his native Rhine Valley. Five years later, he bought land with Frederick and began excavating the hillsides to create tunnels for aging his wines. The brothers founded Beringer Vineyards in 1876. During the building of the caves and winery, Jacob lived in an 1848 farmhouse now known as the Hudson House. The meticulously restored and expanded structure now serves as Beringer Vineyards' Culinary Arts Center.

But the star attraction on the lavishly landscaped grounds is unquestionably the seventeen-room Rhine House, which Frederick modeled after his ancestral home in Germany. The redwood, brick, and stucco mansion is painted in the original Tudor color scheme of earth tones, and slate covers the gabled roof and exterior. The interior of the Rhine House is graced with myriad gems of craftsmanship such as Belgian art nouveau–style stained-glass windows.

The winery's standard tour encompasses a visit to the cellars and the hand-dug aging tunnels in the Old Stone Winery, where tasting is available. Beringer also offers programs that provide visitors more in-depth experiences. The Vintage Legacy Tour, focusing on the winery's history, takes guests to the original St. Helena Home Vineyard, then to the Old Stone Winery for a barrel tasting, and finally to the Cellar Tasting Room to sample additional wines. The Taste of Beringer Tour covers the growing cycle of a grapevine and proceeds through the Old Stone Winery. The Family Tour, which includes sampling Beringer wines, takes visitors through the aging tunnels.

BERINGER VINEYARDS
2000 Main St.
St. Helena, CA 94574
707-963-4812
www.beringer.com

OWNER: Treasury Wine Estates.

LOCATION: On Hwy. 29 about .5 mile north of St. Helena.

APPELLATION: Napa Valley.

HOURS: 10 A.M.–5 P.M. daily in winter; until 6 P.M. in summer.

TASTINGS AND TOURS: Various options are available. Check www.beringer.com for information and reservations.

THE WINES: Cabernet Sauvignon, Chardonnay, Merlot, Pinot Noir, Sauvignon Blanc.

SPECIALTIES: Private Reserve Cabernet Sauvignon, single-vineyard Cabernet Sauvignon, Private Reserve Chardonnay.

WINEMAKER: Laurie Hook.

ANNUAL PRODUCTION: Unavailable.

OF SPECIAL NOTE: Tour includes visit to barrel storage caves hand-chiseled in late 1800s.

NEARBY ATTRACTIONS: Bothe-Napa State Park (hiking, picnicking, horseback riding, swimming Memorial Day–Labor Day); Silverado Museum (Robert Louis Stevenson memorabilia).

CHIMNEY ROCK WINERY

CHIMNEY ROCK WINERY
5350 Silverado Trail
Napa, CA 94558
800-257-2641
707-257-2641
info@chimneyrock.com
www.chimneyrock.com

OWNERS: Terlato family.

LOCATION: 3 miles south of Yountville.

APPELLATION: Stags Leap District.

HOURS: 10 A.M.–5 P.M. daily.

TASTINGS: $20–$25 for 4 wines; $30 for 5 reserve wines. Ganymede Tasting with wine and cheese ($50) daily by appointment.

TOURS: Estate tour and tasting ($35), Elevage tour and tasting ($70), and Vineyard tour and tasting ($90) offered daily by appointment.

THE WINES: Cabernet Franc, Cabernet Sauvignon, Merlot, Petit Verdot, Sauvignon Blanc, Sauvignon Gris.

SPECIALTIES: 100 percent estate-grown Stags Leap District Cabernet Sauvignon, Elevage (red Bordeaux blend), Elevage Blanc (white Bordeaux blend).

WINEMAKER: Elizabeth Vianna.

ANNUAL PRODUCTION: 30,000 cases.

OF SPECIAL NOTE: Picnic area. Annual Vineyard to Vintner event (April) by Stags Leap District winegrowers. Winery is pet friendly. Limited-production, single-vineyard wines available in tasting room only. Gift shop with original paintings, stemware, and Arte Italica serving pieces.

NEARBY ATTRACTIONS: Napa Valley Museum (winemaking displays, art exhibits), Napa Valley Opera House (live performances in historic building).

A quarter mile past the elegant wrought iron gates of Chimney Rock Winery, the broad face of the winery gleams beyond converging rows of meticulously farmed Cabernet Sauvignon vines. Whitewashed walls, arched doorways, and soaring gables define and distinguish the eye-catching architecture. Marking the eastern border of the Stags Leap District, the oak-studded Vaca Range is a dramatic backdrop for the winery and harbors the volcanic formation that gave the winery its name.

In 1980 Sheldon "Hack" Wilson, after multiple business successes, turned his talents and resources to making great wines. He, along with his wife, Stella, bought a pristine 185-acre property just south of Yountville and promptly planted 74 acres of Cabernet Sauvignon. By 1990 the couple had completed the tasting room and adjacent winery in the Cape Dutch style of Stella's native South Africa. For the winery's facade, the Wilsons commissioned a decorative frieze of Ganymede—cupbearer to the mythical gods of ancient Greece—which gives the building a timeless, old-world feel. An avid gardener and horticulturist, Stella designed and planted elaborate beds surrounding their home and the winery. The abundant gardens continue to flourish today.

In 2000 the Wilsons partnered with the Terlato family, whose participation in the wine industry had spanned more than fifty years and eleven wine-producing countries. Under the care and guidance of Tony, Bill, and John Terlato, an additional 60 acres were planted to Cabernet Sauvignon, and a new state-of-the-art winery facility was built. After Hack Wilson's death, the Terlato family assumed full ownership of the winery, a gem that includes 119 acres of vineyard devoted almost entirely to the winery's signature: Bordeaux varietals. Over the past decade, the Terlato family has carried the winery and its legacy forward by continuing to produce handcrafted, small-production, single-vineyard wines.

Inside the tasting room, natural light pouring through large windows illuminates paintings of the Chimney Rock vineyards, and banners announce the dozens of notable ratings earned by Chimney Rock wines over the years. From behind the oak wine bar, staffers warmly greet guests. Out back, a patio with tables and chairs set under a wisteria-draped arbor is perfect for picnics. From here, visitors can admire Ganymede, the gardens, and, beyond the old winery, the Stags Leap Palisades. To the east is the V-shaped formation where an indigenous Wappo hunter once reported seeing a legendary stag make a diversionary leap to save its herd from flying arrows.

CLOS DU VAL

That this winery has a French name is not an affectation. Owner and cofounder John Goelet's mother was a direct descendant of Françoise Guestier, a native of Bordeaux who worked for the Marquis de Segur, owner of Chateau Lafite and Latour. Clos Du Val translates as "small vineyard estate of a small valley," a modest nomenclature for a winery of its stature.

When Goelet, who is also the son of an American entrepreneur, set out on a global search for premium vineyard land, he found the ideal partner in Bernard Portet. Born in Cognac and raised in Bordeaux, Portet is a descendant of six generations of winemakers. He followed his passion with formal studies at the French winemaking schools of Toulouse and Montpelier before Goelet hired him in 1970 to establish Clos Du Val.

Portet spent two years searching six continents before getting a taste of the Napa Valley climate—or, technically, its microclimates. At the time, the cool evenings and dramatic terrain of the Stags Leap District were relatively undiscovered by winemakers. Goelet proved his faith in Portet by promptly acquiring 150 acres of land in the district. The first vintage of the new venture was a 1972 Cabernet Sauvignon, one of only six California Cabernets selected for the now-legendary Paris tasting in 1976, an event that put the world on notice that Napa Valley was a winemaking force to watch. Ten years later, the same vintage took first place in a rematch, further enhancing Clos Du Val's reputation for creating wines that stand the test of time.

In 1973 Clos Du Val purchased 180 acres in another little-recognized appellation—Carneros in southern Napa. Thirteen years later, the winery released its first Carneros Chardonnay, and four years later, its first Carneros Pinot Noir.

A driveway lined with cypress trees leads to the imposing, vine-covered stone winery, behind which the dramatic rock outcroppings of Stags Leap rise in sharp relief. In front of the tasting room are Mediterranean-style gardens, a raised lawn area with tables and chairs defined by a hedge of boxwood, and a demonstration vineyard with twenty rows of Merlot grapevines, accompanied by brief explanations of vineyard management techniques. Inside the winery, halogen lights on the high ceiling beam down on the wooden tasting bar, the unglazed earth-toned tile floor, and a corner display of merchandise bearing the winery's distinctive, curlicued logo. Glass doors on the far side look into a large fermentation room filled with oak and steel tanks. Visitors are welcome to prolong their visit by playing *pétanque* or enjoying a picnic in the olive grove.

CLOS DU VAL
5330 Silverado Trail
Napa, CA 94558
707-261-5200
800-993-9463
cdv@closduval.com
www.closduval.com

OWNER: John Goelet.

LOCATION: 5 miles north of the town of Napa.

APPELLATION: Napa Valley.

HOURS: 10 A.M.–5 P.M. daily.

TASTINGS: $10 for 4 wines (applicable to wine purchase); $20 for reserve wines.

TOURS: By appointment.

THE WINES: Cabernet Sauvignon, Chardonnay, Merlot, Pinot Noir.

SPECIALTY: Cabernet Sauvignon.

WINEMAKER: John Clews.

ANNUAL PRODUCTION: 65,000 cases.

OF SPECIAL NOTE: *Pétanque* court and picnic areas. Reserve wines available only in the tasting room.

NEARBY ATTRACTIONS: Napa Valley Opera House (live performances in historic building); Napa Valley Museum (winemaking displays, art exhibits).

DOMAINE CARNEROS

DOMAINE CARNEROS
1240 Duhig Rd.
Napa, CA 94559
800-716-BRUT (2788)
707-257-0101
www.domainecarneros.com

OWNERS: Partnership between Taittinger and Kopf families.

LOCATION: Intersection of Hwys. 121/12 and Duhig Rd., 4 miles southwest of the town of Napa and 6 miles southeast of Sonoma.

APPELLATION: Los Carneros.

HOURS: 10 A.M.–6 P.M. daily.

TASTINGS: $7–$15 per glass, depending on variety; $15 for sampler of 3 sparkling wines or $15 for 3 Pinot Noirs.

TOURS: 11 A.M., 1 P.M., and 3 P.M. daily. Group tours for 10 or more by appointment. Additional tours available seasonally.

THE WINES: Brut Rosé, Le Rêve, Pinot Noir, Vintage Brut.

SPECIALTIES: *Méthode champenoise* sparkling wine, Pinot Noir.

WINEMAKERS: Eileen Crane, founding winemaker; T. J. Evans, Pinot Noir winemaker.

ANNUAL PRODUCTION: 48,000 cases.

OF SPECIAL NOTE: Table service in salon or on terrace with panoramic views of Carneros region. Cheese and caviar available for purchase.

NEARBY ATTRACTIONS: di Rosa Preserve (indoor and outdoor exhibits of works by contemporary Bay Area artists); Napa Valley Opera House.

An architectural tribute to its French heritage, the chateau that houses Domaine Carneros would look at home in Champagne, France. It dominates a hillside in the renowned Carneros region in southern Napa, prime growing area for the grape varieties that go into the best sparkling wine and sumptuous Pinot Noir. The opulent winery is approached by a long series of steps that climb to a grand entranceway. French marble floors, high ceilings, and decorative features such as a Louis XV fireplace mantel imbue the interior with a palatial ambience. Guests are welcome to order wines in the elegant salon, warmed by a fireplace on cool days, or on the terrace.

Established in 1987, as a joint venture between France and Kobrand Corporation. President Director-General Claude Taittinger led the extensive search for the ideal site for making world-class sparkling wine. The Carneros region's long, moderately cool growing season and the fog that mitigates the summer heat allow for slow, even ripening and perfect acidic balance in the Pinot Noir and Chardonnay grapes. Domaine Carneros farms four vineyards totaling 350 hundred acres in the appellation. Domaine Carneros began Champagne Taittinger of

Harvest at Domaine Carneros begins in mid-August, when workers head out to pick grapes before dawn. A delicate balance of sugar and acidity is required for the best sparkling wine. The fruit is immediately brought to the press for the gentle extracting of the juice. From that moment through vinification, each lot is maintained separately before the exact blend is determined. The sparkling wines are made in accordance with the traditional *méthode champenoise*, in which secondary fermentation takes place in the bottle, not the tank. The grapes for Pinot Noir are gathered several weeks after the sparkling wine harvest is complete, then are fermented for ten days. After this, the juices are siphoned off, and the fruit is gently pressed to extract the remaining juice. The resulting wine is aged in French oak barrels for up to ten months before bottling.

In charge of these elaborate procedures is president Eileen Crane, who began her career at Domaine Chandon and later served as winemaker and vice president of Gloria Ferrer Champagne Caves in nearby Sonoma. This experience made her the ideal choice for overseeing the planning and development of Domaine Carneros. Crane focuses on making the most of the winery's combination of exceptional vineyards and meticulous winemaking. Early in 2008, she achieved another milestone: Domaine Carneros became the first sparkling winery in the United States to have 100 percent of its estate vineyards certified as organic.

DUCKHORN VINEYARDS

A visit to Duckhorn Vineyards begins at the Estate House, a Victorian-style farmhouse featuring wood siding, white trim, and a wide, welcoming porch. Built in the early 1990s, the gracious structure evokes a nineteenth-century Napa Valley home, complete with wraparound veranda and views of forested hills, the oak-lined banks of the Napa River, and Dan and Margaret Duckhorn's first vineyard, originally planted in 1981.

Over the years, the property has supported a pig farm, a walnut orchard, and a vineyard consulting company that produced grafted grapevines for winegrowers. The Duckhorns discovered the site in 1971, when Dan, who has a background in finance, became general manager of the vineyard consulting company. Five years later, the couple partnered with three other families to purchase the ten-acre estate and establish Duckhorn Vineyards.

The lobby of the Estate inn. Along with armchairs and a with dozens of hand-carved duck pintails, and teals, some dating House evokes an elegant country granite fireplace, it is furnished decoys representing mallards, from the early 1900s. Showcased throughout the tasting room are duck sculptures and paintings, a massive jade duck in flight, and a mural of a wetlands scene—all part of the winery's impressive collection of waterfowl art.

Guests pass a glass-paned wine cellar and circular bar, before taking seats on the veranda or at window-side tables in a room bathed in soft light filtering through ash and dogwood trees. Wines are served in separate glasses to allow side-by-side comparison, and bonus pours include Pinot Noir, a rarity in Bordeaux-centric Napa Valley, from the winery's sister facility in Mendocino County's Anderson Valley.

In the late 1970s, Cabernet Sauvignon and Bordeaux-style blends dominated the wines of Napa Valley, but after traveling to the St. Émilion and Pomerol regions of Bordeaux, Dan Duckhorn decided to focus on Merlot. In 1978 when the Duckhorns released their first vintage—800 cases each of Merlot and Cabernet Sauvignon—the silky texture and early drinkability of their Merlot launched an unprecedented and enduring appreciation for the grape as a stand-alone variety.

A stroll around the grounds reveals winding paths that encourage exploration of gardens billowing with grasses, herbs, and perennials. The drizzle of a millstone fountain signals the location of a secluded patio. Nearby, half barrels display soil from vineyards that provide the winery's fruit. One holds fist-sized rocks from the rugged Three Palms Vineyard, located a few miles north on Silverado Trail and the source of Duckhorn Vineyard's esteemed 1978 Merlot.

DUCKHORN VINEYARDS
1000 Lodi Ln.
St. Helena, CA 94574
707-967-2005
888-354-8885
concierge@duckhorn.com
www.duckhorn.com

OWNER: Duckhorn Wine Company.

LOCATION: At the corner of Lodi Ln. and Silverado Trail, 3 miles north of St. Helena.

APPELLATIONS: St. Helena, Napa Valley.

HOURS: 10 A.M.–4 P.M. daily.

TASTINGS: Essentials Tasting, $15 for 4 current wines. Enhanced Tasting, $25 for 5 limited-production and/or estate-grown wines. Reservations preferred.

TOURS: By appointment. Estate Tour and Tasting ($35), 11 A.M. and 2 P.M. daily. Taste of Terroir, single-vineyard tasting with tour ($45), 2 P.M. daily. Food for Thought Pairing ($55), 11 A.M. daily.

THE WINES: Cabernet Sauvignon, The Discussion (Bordeaux blend), Merlot, Sauvignon Blanc, Semillon.

SPECIALTY: Merlot.

WINEMAKER: Bill Nancarrow.

ANNUAL PRODUCTION: 75,000 cases.

OF SPECIAL NOTE: Extensive collection of waterfowl art. Food-and-wine pairings by reservation. Annual Spring Celebration in May. Cabernet Franc available in tasting room only. One-bottle limit on The Discussion.

NEARBY ATTRACTIONS: Bothe-Napa Valley State Park; Bale Grist Mill State Historic Park; Culinary Institute at Greystone (cooking demonstrations); Silverado Museum (Robert Louis Stevenson memorabilia).

EHLERS ESTATE

EHLERS ESTATE
3222 Ehlers Ln.
St. Helena, CA 94574
707-963-5972
info@ehlersestate.com
www.ehlersestate.com

OWNER: Leducq Foundation.

LOCATION: 3 miles north of St. Helena.

APPELLATION: St. Helena.

HOURS: 9:30 A.M.–4:30 P.M. daily

TASTINGS: Ehlers Salon, $25 for 4 tastes paired with cheeses and bread sticks, daily, 9:30 A.M.–4:30 P.M. Food-and-wine pairing, $50 for vineyard and cellar tour, tasting of barrel samples, and flight of 4 wines paired with small bites, Tuesday–Friday, 9:30 A.M. and 11:30 A.M.

TOURS: Offered with food-and-wine pairing.

THE WINES: Cabernet Franc, Cabernet Sauvignon, Merlot, Sauvignon Blanc.

SPECIALTY: Cabernet Sauvignon "1886."

WINEMAKER: Kevin Morrisey.

ANNUAL PRODUCTION: 8,000 cases.

OF SPECIAL NOTE: Cabernet Franc available only in the tasting room. Shaded picnic area. All winery profits benefit Leducq Foundation.

NEARBY ATTRACTIONS: Culinary Institute of America at Greystone (cooking demonstrations); Bothe-Napa State Park (hiking, picnicking, horse-back riding, swimming Memorial Day–Labor Day); Bale Grist Mill State Historic Park (water-powered mill circa 1846); Silverado Museum (Robert Louis Stevenson memorabilia).

Just off Highway 29, at the end of a country road, Ehlers Estate offers a glimpse into the rural heart of Napa Valley. At the entrance, an antique grape press atop a stone base towers eight feet tall beside olive trees planted more than a century ago. Beyond lie a demonstration vineyard, a raised-bed vegetable garden, and a sculpture of brightly painted grapevines. Low rock walls, oaks, and the winery itself sit at the center of one of Napa Valley's rare, contiguous estate vineyards. Consisting primarily of Cabernet Sauvignon, the vineyard is certified organic and biodynamically farmed. All the fruit is estate grown, giving the winemaker full control from vine to bottle.

Ehlers Estate boasts both a modern winemaking facility and a nineteenth-century winery, built in 1886 of tuff and basalt and cur-  rently serving as the tasting room. Etched above the arched doorway, builder Bernard Ehlers's name can still be seen. A Sacramento grocer, Ehlers bought the property from a viticulturist who had lost his vines to phylloxera. He replanted the vineyard, and after his death in 1901, the winery operated under a variety of names until 1958. In 1987 French entrepreneur and philanthropist Jean Leducq and his wife, Sylviane, purchased seven acres of Ehlers's original holdings and restored the Ehlers name to the property. Over the next four years, they acquired thirty-five more acres to create the estate.

Leducq grew up in Paris and in 1968 took over his grandfather's linen service. Thirty years later, it ranked as the largest family-owned company in France. After suffering a heart attack in the 1970s, Leducq—whose father and grandfather succumbed to heart disease—sought treatment at the Mayo Clinic. When he sold his company in 1996, he started the Leducq Foundation to fund international cardiovascular research. Upon his death in 2002, he left Ehlers Estate in trust to the foundation.

In 2009 Kevin Morrisey, former winemaker at Napa Valley's historic Stags' Leap Winery, became the estate's winemaker. Morrisey, who holds a master's degree in enology and interned at Pomerol's legendary Château Pétrus, spent nearly ten years at Stags' Leap and during his tenure there confirmed his reputation for making complex, *terroir*-driven wines.

Inside the stone winery, a mix of modern café tables, wooden banquet tables, and matching chairs accommodates visitors as they enjoy the winery's signature seated tastings. Bentwood chandeliers hold incandescent candles, and the exposed rock walls, deep-set windows, and side staircase evoke the old west. Relaxed and informative, tastings include food pairings ranging from gourmet cheeses and bread sticks to elaborate bites such as grilled flank steak with black olive chutney, roasted beet and bing cherry gazpacho with smoked blue cheese, and wild cherry chocolates.

ENVY WINES

What's the story behind the name of this winery? Why Envy? According to cofounder Mark Carter, he and partner Nils Venge considered calling it simply NV. That would be catchy, with its clever reference to Napa Valley, as well as the term nonvintage, which is applied to wines blended from two or more different years. A trendy restaurant in downtown Napa called itself NV, but it went belly-up after less than two years in business. That didn't seem a good omen. Since many people who visit Napa are envious of the wine country lifestyle, spelling out the name Envy struck the partners as a better option.

Mark Carter, a native Californian who owns two inns and a restaurant in Eureka, gained a reputation in wine circles more  than a decade ago, when his stellar wine list was selected seven years in a row as a recipient of a Grand Award from *Wine Spectator* magazine. Carter went so far as to convert one of the prized rooms in his Hotel Carter into a cellar to accommodate his vast collection of fine vintages.

Carter and Venge crossed paths in the early 1980s when Venge appeared at the hotelier's very first winemaker dinner. By then, Nils Venge was a well-known figure in Napa Valley and beyond. As a vintner, grape grower, and consultant to many start-up wineries, Venge has been planting, pruning, crushing, fermenting, blending, and bottling in various vineyards and wineries since launching his career at Charles Krug Winery and Sterling Vineyards in the early 1970s. In 1976 he established his own label, Saddleback Cellars, which is located off Oakville Cross Road on a little lane called Money Road.

They never dreamed they would wind up as partners in a new wine venture in Calistoga, but by 1998, as Carter tells the story, he convinced Venge to help him produce wines under the Carter Cellars label. The wines they made regularly garnered more than ninety points from the *Wine Enthusiast* and *Wine & Spirits* as well as *Wine Spectator*. The wines, which carried the names of various notable vineyards (including Napa's esteemed To Kalon and Truchard vineyards) on the label, were produced in small lots, mostly between seventy-five and two hundred cases.

Eventually, the hotelier and the wine guru realized it was time to buy land with a vineyard on it. A two-year search of every available piece of property in Napa Valley led them to a site once occupied by Calistoga Cellars. They bought the existing winery and its adjacent eleven-plus acres of estate vineyards, planted to Cabernet Sauvignon, Merlot, and Petite Sirah. A two-story residential-looking structure washed in ocher now houses Envy's winery and tasting room, which opened in March of 2007.

ENVY WINES
1170 Tubbs Ln.
Calistoga, CA 94515
707-942-4670
info@envywines.com
www.envywines.com

OWNERS: Mark Carter
and Nils Venge.

LOCATION: About 4 miles
north of Calistoga
via Hwy. 128 or the
Silverado Trail.

APPELLATIONS: Calistoga,
Napa Valley.

HOURS: 10 A.M.–4:30 P.M.
daily.

TASTINGS: $10 for 4 or
5 wines.

TOURS: None.

THE WINES: Cabernet
Sauvignon, Merlot, Petite
Sirah, Sauvignon Blanc.

SPECIALTIES: Bee Bee's
Blend (Bordeaux-style
blend or estate blend),
Petite Sirah.

WINEMAKER: Nils Venge.

ANNUAL PRODUCTION:
1,800 cases.

OF SPECIAL NOTE:
Guests may picnic
on outdoor tables
surrounding the tasting
room, with panoramic
views of the Palisades and
Old Faithful Geyser. Two
other labels are available
at Envy: Vine Haven and
Carter Cellars wines.

NEARBY ATTRACTIONS:
Old Faithful Geyser
of California; Petrified
Forest (walking trails
through Pliocene fossil
forest formed by volcanic
action); Robert Louis
Stevenson State Park
(hiking).

ETUDE WINES

ETUDE WINES
1250 Cuttings Wharf Rd.
Napa, CA 94558
707-257-5300
info@etudewines.com
www.etudewines.com

OWNER: Treasury Wine Estates.

LOCATION: About 4 miles southwest of the town of Napa.

APPELLATION: Los Carneros.

HOURS: 10 A.M.–4:30 P.M. daily.

TASTINGS: $15 for 5 wines; $25 for 5 reserve wines by appointment. Wine-and-food pairings, $35 for 6 wines and 3 savory bites, 10 A.M., 1 P.M., and 3 P.M., Friday–Sunday, by appointment

TOURS: None.

THE WINES: Cabernet Sauvignon, Chardonnay, Pinot Blanc, Pinot Gris, Pinot Noir.

SPECIALTIES: Chardonnay, Napa Valley Cabernet, estate Pinot Noir.

WINEMAKER: Jon Priest.

ANNUAL PRODUCTION: 28,000 cases.

OF SPECIAL NOTE: Picnic tables available with advance reservations. Winery is pet friendly. Winery holds summer educational series. Rutherford and Oakville Cabernet Sauvignon, Pinot Blanc, and Temblor Pinot Noir available in tasting room only.

NEARBY ATTRACTIONS: di Rosa Preserve (indoor and outdoor exhibits of works by contemporary Bay Area artists); Napa Valley Opera House (live performances in historic building).

Napa Valley is renowned for its rugged foothills and sun-drenched vineyards, but in its southwestern reaches, visitors find lush, naturally occurring wetlands. Part of the Carneros appellation, this secluded corner supports scores of birds, including egrets, herons, and geese, as well as mature stands of oaks and California bay trees. Here, the marine influence from nearby San Pablo Bay moderates summer heat, helping to extend the growing season for Pinot Noir, Etude's signature wine. Unlike the sedimentary clay under most Carneros vineyards, the soils of Etude's 1,300-acre property are rocky, well drained, and volcanic, making them ideal for growing Burgundian varieties. Planted to conform to the changing topography, Etude's vineyard rows run at diverse angles, and blocks average only eight acres. Close spacing of the vines produces low yields of highly flavorful fruit. With four protected wetlands on the property, winery workers take extra care to farm sustainably and keep waterways clean.

Etude Wines was founded in 1980 by winemaker Tony Soter, who envisioned a wine-growing house where improved vineyard practices reduced the need for vinicultural intervention. Soter began his career at Stag's Leap Wine Cellars and was an early champion of crafting wines that expressed the characteristics of individual vineyards. He preferred to buy grapes by the acre, rather than by the ton, which motivated growers to reduce their yields and produce better fruit. The winery released its first Napa Valley Cabernet Sauvignon in 1980 and continues to source fruit from prime Cabernet Sauvignon benchlands located in Napa Valley, including the Rutherford, Oakville, St. Helena, and Calistoga appellations.

With the release of its first Carneros Pinot Noir in 1982, the winery launched its acclaimed Pinot Noir program, which includes a seven-acre estate vineyard dedicated to rare clones of the grape. In 2005, winemaker Jon Priest moved from the California Central Coast wine region to practice his craft alongside Soter. Priest had worked for more than a dozen years at Wild Horse Winery, where he made more than thirty varieties before moving to Adelaida Cellars, and then to TAZ Vineyards in 2003. One of the few winemakers to attend college on a steeplechase scholarship, Priest harbors a special fondness for Pinot Noir, savoring the challenges posed by the finicky grape, as well as the pure pleasure it delivers when handled correctly.

In 2009 Etude Wines opened a new tasting room, an elegant space with blond oak paneling and an intricately patterned floor made from end-cut Douglas fir. Embedded rice hulls add a pleasant texture to the concrete tasting bar, and on the wall behind it, a backlit rack holds rows of wine bottles that glow like colorful works of art.

FRANK FAMILY VINEYARDS

At a time when many Napa Valley wineries are increasingly exclusive, the convivial, unpretentious ambience at Frank Family Vineyards is decidedly refreshing. Yet this is not the only reason for heading slightly off the beaten path to reach this historic property. The Frank Family Vineyards wines are made in a massive stone building first constructed in 1884 as Larkmead Winery, the third oldest winery in Napa. Refurbished in 1906 with sandstone from the nearby hills, the structure is listed on the National Register of Historic Places and as an official Point of Historical Interest in the state of California.

In 1992 Rich Frank had the opportunity to purchase the Kornell Champagne Cellars at Larkmead Winery. A sentimental guy at heart, Frank continues to produce sparkling wines in the old cellar where thick stone walls, high-stacked barrels, and the unmistakable bouquet of aging wines impart an almost palpable sense of history. Winemaker Todd Graff, who was previously a winemaker at Schramsberg, handcrafts Blanc de Blancs, Blanc de Noirs, Rouge, and Reserve in the traditional French *méthode champenoise* style. Visitors can see the equipment Graff uses to produce 2,200 cases of sparkling wine each year.

The focus at Frank Family Vineyards, however, is largely on still wines, using grapes from three distinguished Napa vineyards. Winston Hill, Rich Frank's personal estate, is situated five hundred feet above the valley floor in Rutherford and produces Cabernet Sauvignon as well as small amounts of Merlot, Cabernet Franc, and Sangiovese. The grapes from this vineyard are used for Frank Family's estate wines—Winston Hill Red Wine, Rutherford Reserve Cabernet, and Rutherford Reserve Sangiovese. Fruit for the winery's Napa Valley Cabernet Sauvignon comes from the SJ Vineyard in the Capell Valley, located east of the Vaca Range. Frank Family's Lewis Vineyard at Buchli Station is in the heart of Carneros, where the combination of cool maritime climate and shallow, dense clay loam soils produces lively, well-balanced Chardonnay and Pinot Noir.

As former president of Disney Studios, Rich Frank knows how to make visitors feel welcome. The tasting room, at times brimming with laughter, is recognized among the best in the country—the May 2008 *Wine Enthusiast* featured it as one of the country's top twenty-five tasting rooms. The winery was voted best in Napa by *San Francisco Chronicle* readers in a 2010 poll. A new tasting room in a remodeled Craftsman house on the property provides separate areas for sampling sparkling wines and still wines. Outside, visitors are welcome to relax at the wooden picnic tables under statuesque elm trees and enjoy the spectacular vineyard views.

FRANK FAMILY VINEYARDS
1091 Larkmead Ln.
Calistoga, CA 94515
800-574-9463
www.frankfamily
vineyards.com

OWNERS: Frank family (Rich, Connie, Paul, Darryl, Vanessa, Lewis, Stella, and Jeremy).

LOCATION: About 5 miles north of St. Helena via Hwy. 29.

APPELLATION: Napa Valley.

HOURS: 10 A.M.–5 P.M. daily.

TASTINGS: $10; $25 for reserve tasting.

TOURS: None.

THE WINES: Cabernet Sauvignon, Chardonnay, Pinot Noir, Sangiovese, sparkling wine, Zinfandel.

SPECIALTIES: Cabernet Sauvignon from Rutherford, Chardonnay, sparkling wine.

WINEMAKER: Todd Graff.

ANNUAL PRODUCTION: 20,000 cases.

OF SPECIAL NOTE: Reserve Lewis Chardonnay, Pinot Noir, Sangiovese, and Zinfandel; Rutherford Reserve Cabernet; Winston Hill Red Wine; and *méthode champenoise* sparkling wines available only at winery.

NEARBY ATTRACTIONS: Bothe-Napa State Park; Robert Louis Stevenson State Park; Old Faithful Geyser of California; Petrified Forest; Sharpsteen Museum (exhibits on Robert Louis Stevenson and Walt Disney animator Ben Sharpsteen).

GRGICH HILLS ESTATE

GRGICH HILLS ESTATE
1829 St. Helena Hwy.
Rutherford, CA 94573
800-532-3057
info@grgich.com
www.grgich.com

OWNERS: Miljenko "Mike" Grgich and Austin Hills.

LOCATION: About 3 miles south of St. Helena.

APPELLATION: Napa Valley.

HOURS: 9:30 A.M.–4:30 P.M. daily.

TASTINGS: $15 for 5 wines.

TOURS: By appointment, 11 A.M. and 2 P.M. daily.

THE WINES: Cabernet Sauvignon, Chardonnay, Fumé Blanc, Merlot, Violetta (late-harvest dessert wine), Zinfandel.

SPECIALTY: Chardonnay.

WINEMAKER: Mike Grgich.

ANNUAL PRODUCTION: 70,000 cases.

OF SPECIAL NOTE: Barrel tastings held 2–4 P.M. on Friday afternoons, except during harvest, when grape stomping is offered daily. Napa Valley Wine Train stops at Grgich Hills for special tour and tasting; call 800-427-4124 for schedule.

NEARBY ATTRACTIONS: Bothe-Napa State Park (hiking, picnicking, horseback riding, swimming Memorial Day–Labor Day); Bale Grist Mill State Historic Park (water-powered mill circa 1846); Silverado Museum (Robert Louis Stevenson memorabilia).

Few people driving along Highway 29 recognize both of the red, white, and blue flags flying in front of this winery. They certainly know one, the American flag. The other represents Croatia, the native country of winemaker and co-owner Miljenko "Mike" Grgich.

The simple red-tile-roofed, white stucco building may not be as flashy as those of nearby wineries, but as the saying goes, it's what's inside that counts. Once visitors pass beneath the grapevine trellis and into the dimly lit recesses of the tasting room, they forget about exterior appearances. The comfortable, old-world atmosphere at Grgich Hills Estate is not a gimmick.

The winery was founded by Mike Grgich (pronounced "GUR-gitch") and Austin E. Hills on July 4, 1977. Both were already well known. Hills is a member of the Hills Brothers coffee family. Grgich was virtually legendary, especially in France. He had drawn worldwide attention in 1976, when, at the now-famous Paris tasting, an all-French panel of judges chose his 1973 Chateau Montelena Chardonnay over the best of the white Burgundies in a

blind tasting. It was a momentous occasion for the California wine industry in general and in particular for Mike Grgich, who was already acknowledged as one of the state's top winemakers.

Finally in a position to capitalize on his fame, Grgich quickly found a simpatico partner in Hills, who had a background in business and finance and was the owner of established vineyards. The two men shortly began turning out the intensely flavored Chardonnays that remain the flagship wines of Grgich Hills Estate.

Grgich, easily recognizable with his trademark blue beret, was born in 1923 into a winemaking family on the Dalmatian coast of Croatia. He arrived in California in 1958 and spent his early years at Beaulieu Vineyard, where he worked with the late, pioneering winemaker André Tchelistcheff before moving on to Mondavi and Chateau Montelena. Grgich continues to make wine and relies on a younger generation—daughter Violet Grgich, vice president of sales and marketing, and nephew Ivo Jeramaz, vice president of production and vineyard development—to carry on the family tradition. Visitors may well run into family members when taking the exceptionally informative winery tour or while sampling wines in the cool, cellarlike tasting room or in the VIP tasting room and hospitality center.

HALL ST. HELENA

Vintners Craig and Kathryn Hall are the kind of people who dream big—and then bring those dreams to life in dramatic fashion. Kathryn Hall had long wanted a chance to continue her family's winemaking heritage and seized the opportunity to take over an existing winery that, despite its historic significance, had been largely overlooked by wine lovers. Her goal was to become known as a seriously dedicated boutique producer of Bordeaux varietals that would express the true character of both the fruit and the land.

The Halls bought the property, which included a tasting room as well as a defunct winemaking facility next door. They dramatically transformed the lackluster tasting room into a destination not only for wine aficionados but also for fans of modern art, and opened Hall St. Helena in 2003. The winery's entrance courtyard is dominated by a seven-foot-tall sculpture, *Moebus Tower*, in the shape of a horizontal figure eight, the symbol of infinity. Painted a vibrant red, the piece inspired the color of the winery's logo. Hall St. Helena also commissioned a number of wine-related sculptures that adorn the grounds. The interior of the tasting room is now an airy, colorful space further brightened by original artwork from the Halls' own collection.

HALL

Cabernet
Sauvignon
2006

Napa Valley

Hall St. Helena, open daily to the public, offers a tour of the property that concludes with a barrel tasting of upcoming vintages, together with a sit-down reserve tasting of current releases. Visitors may also ask to see the adjacent historic stone winery that was built in 1885 by New England sea captain William Peterson, the first of several owners over the next century.

The Halls may respect their winery's storied past, but their focus is on the future. They farm all their vineyards organically, and even more notably, Hall St. Helena is the first winery in California to achieve LEED Gold certification. LEED (Leadership in Energy and Environmental Design) acknowledges outstanding examples of environmentally sensitive design elements and energy-saving features such as radiant flooring and solar power. Another point of pride is that Hall St. Helena reuses 100 percent of its water supply.

Following the first two phases of ambitious renovations—the transformation of the tasting room and grounds and the LEED qualification improvements—the Halls will begin the third phase in 2011. The warehouse structure that has obscured the 1885 facility for many decades will be torn down so that the old building can be seen once again. The Halls will then surround the historic winery with a courtyard and organic garden to highlight their environmental commitment and celebrate the senses.

HALL ST. HELENA
401 St. Helena Hwy. South
St. Helena, CA 94574
707-967-2626
celebrate@hallwines.com
www.hallwines.com

OWNERS: Craig and
Kathryn Hall.

LOCATION: About 2 miles
south of St. Helena.

APPELLATION: Napa Valley.

HOURS: 10 A.M.–5:30 P.M.
daily.

TASTINGS: $15 for Artisan
Tasting of 4 small-
production wines; $25 for
Premium Cabernet Tasting
of 2 estate Cabernets.

TOURS: By appointment,
11 A.M. and 1 P.M. daily.
Includes barrel tasting
($30) or added pairing
of wine with artisan
cheese ($45).

THE WINES: Cabernet
Sauvignon, Merlot,
Sauvignon Blanc.

SPECIALTY: Bordeaux
varietals.

WINEMAKER: Steve Leveque.

ANNUAL PRODUCTION:
40,000 cases.

OF SPECIAL NOTE: Winery
displays owners' collection
of contemporary art. A
number of picnic areas
available in a mulberry
tree–shaded arbor
adjacent to the tasting
room. A second winery,
Hall Rutherford, is open
only by appointment.

NEARBY ATTRACTIONS:
Bothe-Napa State Park
(hiking, picnicking,
horseback riding,
swimming Memorial
Day–Labor Day); Bale
Grist Mill State Historic
Park (water-powered
mill circa 1846); Silverado
Museum (Robert Louis
Stevenson memorabilia).

HEITZ WINE CELLARS

HEITZ WINE CELLARS
Tasting and Sales Room:
436 St. Helena Hwy. South
St. Helena, CA 94574
707-963-3542
Mailing Address:
500 Taplin Rd.
St. Helena, CA 94574
www.heitzcellar.com

OWNERS: Heitz family.

LOCATION: 2 miles south of
St. Helena.

APPELLATION: Napa Valley.

HOURS: 11 A.M.–4:30 P.M.
daily.

TASTINGS: Complimentary.

TOURS: Of winery by
appointment.

THE WINES: Cabernet
Sauvignon, Chardonnay,
Grignolino, Port, Sauvignon
Blanc, Zinfandel.

SPECIALTIES: Vineyard-
designated Cabernet
Sauvignon.

WINEMAKERS: David Heitz,
Joe Norman.

ANNUAL PRODUCTION:
40,000 cases.

OF SPECIAL NOTE: The only
Napa Valley producer of
Grignolino, a red Italian
wine grape commonly
grown in the Piedmont
region.

NEARBY ATTRACTIONS:
Culinary Institute of
America at Greystone
(cooking demonstrations);
Bothe-Napa State Park
(hiking, picnicking,
horseback riding,
swimming Memorial
Day–Labor Day); Bale Grist
Mill State Historic Park
(water-powered mill circa
1846); Silverado Museum
(Robert Louis Stevenson
memorabilia).

Among Napa Valley's few midcentury wineries to remain independent, Heitz Wine Cellars consistently produces internationally acclaimed Cabernet Sauvignon. Marking the winery's fiftieth anniversary in 2011, the Heitz family celebrates the enduring legacy of Joe Heitz, among the most influential winemakers of his time, and the label that he and his wife, Alice, founded in 1961.

Heitz, who received a bachelor's degree in enology in 1948, worked with renowned winemaker André Tchelistcheff at Beaulieu Vineyard for seven years. In 1958, he earned a master's degree in food science and became the first enology professor at Fresno State University. Eager to return to Napa Valley, the Heitzes bought an eight-acre vineyard with a winery and two small houses, located two miles south of St. Helena, on Highway 29. The family lived in one of the homes and opened the winery's first sales center in the other. By 1964, having outgrown the property, the Heitzes purchased a 160-acre ranch and residence on Taplin Road, two miles east of St. Helena, in the hills just off the Silverado Trail. The ranch included a farmhouse and a chiseled perlite winery erected in 1898 by Anton Rossi, a Swiss-Italian vintner. The Heitz family eventually built a modern production facility but continues to use Rossi's old stone structure for extended barrel aging.

After meeting Cabernet Sauvignon growers Tom and Martha May, who own Martha's Vineyard in Oakville, Heitz crafted such a remarkable wine from their 1966 vintage that the two families put the vineyard's name on the label, becoming the first in Napa Valley to embrace vineyard designation. Heitz Wine Cellars continues to craft Cabernet Sauvignon from Martha's Vineyard, which reigns as one of the most widely recognized in the world.

The winery entered the twenty-first century with second-generation Kathleen Heitz Myers as president, and her brother David as winemaker. The dynamic sibling team has helped build the winery's distinguished reputation. In 2002 the family replaced the original sales center on Highway 29 with a tasting room built of native stone and including a tasting bar whose block of polished mahogany atop low concrete pillars recalls the plank-and-barrel days of early tasting rooms. On a back patio, water cascades over a millstone fountain, and visitors can admire panoramic views of a twelve-acre vineyard—the first Cabernet Sauvignon planted by the Heitzes. Like all the Heitz estate vineyards, it is organically and sustainably farmed. Blooming among the coral bells and lavender are irises, Joe's favorite, planted in tribute to the master winemaker, who passed away in 2000.

THE HESS COLLECTION WINERY

A gently winding road heads up a forested mountainside to this winery on the western rim of the Napa Valley. Although only a fifteen-minute drive from bustling Highway 29, the estate feels a thousand times removed. Arriving visitors are greeted with stunning vineyard views from almost every vantage point.

Swiss entrepreneur Donald Hess has owned vineyards on Mount Veeder since 1978, so when he decided to establish his own winery, he didn't have to look far to find the Christian Brothers Mont La Salle property. He already knew that the east side of the extinct volcano provides a cool climate that allows a long growing season as well as excellent soil drainage—two viticultural components known for producing Cabernet Sauvignon with excellent structure and superb con- centration of aromas and flavors. Vineyards were first planted on this land in the 1860s, long before the ivy-clad, three-story stone winery was built in 1903. The Christian Brothers produced wine here for nearly a half century before leasing the facilities to Hess in 1986. He began planting Cabernet Sauvignon vineyards on terrain so steep they have to be picked by hand. The vines must grow extended roots to cling to the mountainside, and the resultant stress creates fruit of exceptional character.

The Hess Collection farms 310 acres of Mount Veeder vineyards that range in elevation from six hundred to two thousand feet. Viewing itself as a steward of the land, the winery farms these vineyards using the principles of sustainable and organic agriculture.

Hess spent three years renovating the facility before opening it to the public in 1989. The overhaul included transforming thirteen thousand square feet on the second and third floors to display his extensive collection of international art, which includes 143 paintings, sculptures, and interactive pieces by modern and contemporary artists including such luminaries as Francis Bacon, Frank Stella, Anselm Kiefer, Andy Goldsworthy, and Robert Motherwell. Two works evoke a particularly strong response for their social commentary. One is Argentinean Leopold Maler's *Hommage 1974*, an eternally burning typewriter created in protest of the repression of artistic freedom. Another is Polish sculptor Magdalena Abakanowicz's *Crowd*, a group of nineteen life-size headless figures made of resin and burlap sacks.

The tasting room, which shares the first floor with a century-old barrel-aging cellar, is built from a local metamorphic sandstone called rhyolite. The stone had been covered with stucco by the Christian Brothers but was inadvertently exposed during the winery's renovation. This is where visitors linger and share their impressions of both the wine and the art.

THE HESS COLLECTION WINERY
4411 Redwood Rd.
Napa, CA 94558
707-255-8584
www.hesscollection.com

FOUNDER: Donald Hess.

LOCATION: 7 miles west of Hwy. 29.

APPELLATIONS: Mount Veeder, Napa Valley.

HOURS: 10 A.M.–5:30 P.M. daily in summer; 10 A.M.–5 P.M. daily in winter.

TASTINGS: $10–$20. Food-and-wine pairings at 10 A.M. and 2 P.M. on Thursday, Friday, and Saturday by reservation.

TOURS: Art collection open daily. Guided tours of winery and collection available.

THE WINES: Cabernet Sauvignon, Chardonnay, 19 Block Cuvée, Petite Sirah, Sauvignon Blanc, Viognier, Zinfandel.

SPECIALTIES: Mount Veeder Cabernet Sauvignon, Chardonnay, 19 Block Cuvée.

WINEMAKERS: David Guffy (Hess), Randle Johnson (Artezin).

ANNUAL PRODUCTION: 90,000 cases.

OF SPECIAL NOTE: Extensive collection of international art. Many wines available only in tasting room.

NEARBY ATTRACTION: Alston Regional Park (hiking).

KULETO ESTATE

KULETO ESTATE
2470 Sage Canyon Rd.
St. Helena, CA 94574
707-963-9750
707-302-2200
info@kuletoestate.com
www.kuletoestate.com

OWNERS: Pat Kuleto and
William P. Foley.

LOCATION: About 10.5 miles
southeast of St. Helena.

APPELLATION: Napa Valley.

HOURS: By appointment
only.

TASTINGS: Part of tour fee.

TOURS: By appointment,
10:30 A.M., 11:45 A.M.,
1 P.M, and 2:30 P.M. daily.
Fee ($35) includes tour,
4 wine samples, and
artisan cheese pairing.

THE WINES: Cabernet
Franc, Cabernet
Sauvignon, Chardonnay,
Moscato, Pinot Noir,
Rosato, Sangiovese, Syrah,
Zinfandel.

SPECIALTY: Cabernet
Sauvignon.

WINEMAKER: Dave Lattin.

ANNUAL PRODUCTION:
8,000 cases.

OF SPECIAL NOTE: The tour
features a guided walk
around the property with
its expansive views of
Lake Hennessey. Dinner
by reservation. Cabernet
Franc, Chardonnay, and
Pinot Noir available only
at winery.

NEARBY ATTRACTION:
Lake Hennessey (boating,
fishing, camping).

Built on virgin land less than twenty years ago, the Tuscan-style villa and winery at the pinnacle of this 761-acre estate could be mistaken for a rustic village perched on an Italian hilltop. In 1992, after culinary entrepreneur Pat Kuleto assembled five parcels from cattle ranchers, he set out to create a serene and sustainable retreat where he could indulge his passion for fine food and wine. An equally important goal was to foster European-style hospitality that would entice friends and wine lovers to the scenic property overlooking Lake Hennessey, Pritchard Hill, and the towns of Rutherford and St. Helena.

Erecting buildings, along with a swimming pool, on relatively flat ground was one thing, but planting grapevines on wild, steep terrain would be quite another. Famed in the food world for fashioning memorable restaurants out of previously unremarkable spaces, Kuleto was undeterred when faced with the challenge of creating world-class vineyards on Napa Valley's eastern mountains.

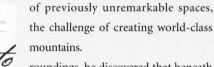
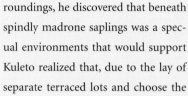

As Kuleto explored his new surroundings, he discovered that beneath the manzanita scrub, chaparral, and spindly madrone saplings was a spectrum of distinct soil types and individual environments that would support a remarkable range of grape varietals. Kuleto realized that, due to the lay of the land, he would have to establish separate terraced lots and choose the rootstocks and clones best suited to each location and orientation. Within a year, he began planting the first wave of varietals, including Cabernet Sauvignon, Chardonnay, Pinot Noir, and Sangiovese. Later would come Muscat, Syrah, Zinfandel, and a handful of other small-lot blending varietals in vineyards established at elevations ranging from 800 to 1,450 feet.

While the grapevines took root and began to mature, Kuleto pursued other aspects of his grand vision for transforming this secluded aerie into a working ranch. He planted fruit orchards and an extensive organic garden and also acquired a menagerie of pigs, ducks, turkeys, rabbits, and sheep. He established ponds around the property and stocked them with sturgeon, catfish, bluegill, and other fish. In all, the estate probably could feed an entire village.

By 2001 construction was completed on the stone-clad winery, designed by Kuleto to blend in with the old-world look of Villa Cucina, his nearby residence. The 17,000-square-foot, gravity-flow facility may look weathered, but it has all the elements winemaker Dave Lattin needs to craft the lots of ultrapremium fruit from each small vineyard block at every stage of development into wine. Visitors can sample the finished product on a covered veranda overlooking the rolling hillsides studded with oaks and madrones.

MARKHAM VINEYARDS

Few people are surprised to hear that Charles Krug, Schramsberg, and Sutter Home wineries were in business in 1874. Less widely known is that they were the only three wineries operating in Napa Valley that year, when Jean Laurent founded the St. Helena winery that, less than a century later, would become known as Markham Vineyards.

Laurent, a Frenchman from Bordeaux, arrived in California in 1852, drawn by the lure of the 1849 Gold Rush. When his prospecting failed to pan out, he made his way to the city of Napa in 1868 and began growing vegetables. Laurent quickly assessed the high quality of the soil and, being from Bordeaux, realized Napa Valley was ideally suited to grapevines. Six years later, he established the Laurent Winery in St. Helena. After Laurent died in 1890, the property changed hands a number of times. In 1977 it was purchased by Bruce Markham, who had already acquired prime vineyard land on the Napa Valley floor, including 93 acres in Yountville once owned by Inglenook. By 1978 he had added the Calistoga Ranch at the headlands of the Napa River and the Oak Knoll Vineyard in the Oak Knoll District. The Markham estate vineyards now cover a total of 330 acres, including the most recent acquisition, Trubody Vineyards, west of Yountville in the center of the valley. These four areas have distinct microclimates that contribute to the complexity of the various wines produced by the winery.

In 1988 the winery and vineyard holdings were sold to Japan's oldest and largest wine company, Mercian Corporation. Despite these changes, many things have remained constant. The current owners have maintained the winery's dedication to producing ultrapremium wines sold at relatively modest prices. The first employee hired by Markham, Bryan Del Bondio, a native of Napa Valley from a family immersed in winemaking, is now president of Markham Vineyards. Jean Laurent's original stone cellar sits at the heart of the facility.

Stylistically, the winery combines both historic and modern elements, with its old stone and concrete facade, and its subdued red metal roofing supported by round wooden columns. Koi ponds flank the approach to the tasting room, and beyond them, orange and yellow canna lilies provide bursts of color when the plants bloom in spring and summer. The tasting room has a large fireplace to warm visitors on cold days and an outdoor terrace to enjoy on sunny days. The Markham Gallery features artwork and photography by noted artists.

MARKHAM VINEYARDS
2812 St. Helena Hwy. North
St. Helena, CA 94574
707-963-5292
www.markhamvineyards.com

OWNER: Mercian Corporation.

LOCATION: 1 mile north of St. Helena on Hwy. 29.

APPELLATION: Napa Valley.

HOURS: 11 A.M.–5 P.M. daily.

TASTINGS: $15–$25 for current releases and library and estate selections.

TOURS: By appointment.

THE WINES: Cabernet Sauvignon, Chardonnay, Merlot, Sauvignon Blanc.

SPECIALTY: Merlot.

WINEMAKER: Kimberlee Jackson Nicholls.

ANNUAL PRODUCTION: 100,000 cases.

OF SPECIAL NOTE: Visitor center, home of the Markham Gallery, hosts ongoing exhibits. Dinners in the historic stone cellar by appointment.

NEARBY ATTRACTIONS: Bothe-Napa State Park (hiking, picnicking, horseback riding, swimming Memorial Day–Labor Day); Bale Grist Mill State Historic Park (water-powered mill circa 1846); Culinary Institute of America at Greystone (cooking demonstrations); Silverado Museum (Robert Louis Stevenson memorabilia).

MUMM NAPA

MUMM NAPA
8445 Silverado Trail
Rutherford, CA 94573
707-967-7700
mumm_info@
mummnapa.com
www.mummnapa.com

OWNER: Pernod Ricard USA.

LOCATION: East of
Rutherford, 1 mile south
of Rutherford Cross Rd.

APPELLATION: Napa Valley.

HOURS: 10 A.M.–5 P.M. daily
(last seating at 4:45 P.M.).

TASTINGS: $10 and up for
flights of 2, or by the flute.

TOURS: 10 A.M., 11 A.M.,
1 P.M., and 3 P.M. daily.

THE WINES: Blanc de Blancs,
Brut Prestige, Brut Rosé,
Demi Sec, DVX, Sparkling
Pinot Noir, Vintage Reserve.

SPECIALTY: Sparkling wine
made in traditional French
style.

WINEMAKER: Ludovic
Dervin.

ANNUAL PRODUCTION:
200,000 cases.

OF SPECIAL NOTE: Exhibits
of internationally known
and local artists. Limited
availability of Chardonnay,
Pinot Gris, and Pinot Noir,
and of large-format bottles,
at winery.

NEARBY ATTRACTIONS:
Napa Valley Museum
(winemaking displays,
art exhibits).

For connoisseurs of Champagne, relaxing outdoors on a sunny day with a glass of bubbly, in the company of good friends, with a panoramic vineyard view may be the ultimate pleasure. This is obviously what the founders of Mumm Napa had in mind when they conceived of establishing a winery in North America that could produce a sparkling wine that would live up to Champagne standards.

In 1979 representatives of Champagne Mumm of France began quietly searching for the ideal location for a winery. So secretive was their project that they even had a code name for it: Project Lafayette. The point man was  the late Guy Devaux, a native of Epernay, the epicenter of France's Champagne district and an expert on *méthode champenoise*. In this French style of winemaking, the wine undergoes its bubble-producing fermentation in the very bottle from which it will be drunk. Devaux crisscrossed the United States for four years before settling on Napa Valley, the country's best-known appellation.

The best way to appreciate Mumm Napa is to start with a tour. The winery has a reputation for putting on one of the best in the business, covering the complicated steps necessary to get all those bubbles into each bottle. The hour-long tour heads first to the demonstration garden, then proceeds to the winery. The best time of year to take the tour is during the harvest season, usually between mid-August and mid-October. However, there is a lot to see at any time of year, and conveniently, the entire tour takes place on one level.

Visitors enter the winery through the wine shop; the tasting veranda is just beyond, with spectacular views of the vineyards and the Mayacamas Range.

Mumm Napa is also noted for its fine art gallery. The winery exhibits the work of many renowned, as well as local, photographers in its expansive gallery. Guests may explore the gallery at their leisure, even while they enjoy a glass of sparkling wine.

PARADUXX

The mustard yellow Paraduxx Vineyard House resembles a classic Napa Valley farmstead, but inside, the décor is strikingly modern. Near a fourteen-foot-tall window, tufted black leather chairs and benches are grouped around a low table, and throughout the T-shaped space, tall chairs with chrome legs and black leather seats surround polished cherry-on-beech cocktail tables. Sunshine spills through an elevated skylight in the vaulted ceiling, and the walls display a gallery of original paintings created for the winery's duck-themed labels.

The Vineyard House was built in 2005 by Duckhorn Wine Company, whose founders, Dan and Margaret Duckhorn, started Duckhorn Vineyards in the mid-1970s. The couple had consistently crafted outstanding Merlot and Cabernet Sauvignon, and by 1994, they were eager to explore other grape varieties. Keen to retain the Bordeaux focus of the Duckhorn brand, they launched a label devoted to blends based on Zinfandel, a grape identified with early California viticulture. They chose the name Paraduxx for its allusion to both their surname and the unorthodox blends they intended to make.

For the first vintage, the Paraduxx team vinified four tons of Zinfandel from the century-old Korte Vineyard, located just north of St. Helena and still owned by the family who operated the property's pre-Prohibition winery. They blended it with Cabernet Sauvignon, Merlot, and Petite Sirah to create a unique wine that they felt rivaled the Super Tuscan and Australian Shiraz blends, while reflecting California's freewheeling originality.

Paraduxx initially offered only one wine. Therefore, staffers poured three vintages to create a multidimensional tasting. As a rare treat, visitors can still taste a vertical flight of the winery's signature Zinfandel/Cabernet Sauvignon blend. Tastings are always seated, and hosts provide plenty of personal attention, as well as paired nibbles, including savory crackers and cheeses such as Vermont's Cabot cheddar and French Mimollette. Label art in the form of collectible cards—with blend, vintage, and sensory profile information on the back—accompanies each wine.

In fair weather, tasters may opt to sit amid the white market umbrellas and black walnut trees behind the tasting room. Private tastings are sometimes conducted in the barrel rooms bracketing the ten-sided fermentation cellar. A stunning structure with a stone veneer foundation, the cellar mimics Northern California's nineteenth-century round barns. Its interior affords easy access to the central wine press and stainless tanks around the perimeter. After harvest, when workers have stowed the press, in its place stands a glistening sculpture of a pair of ducks.

PARADUXX
7257 Silverado Trail
Napa, CA 94558
707-945-0890
866-367-9943
tastings@paraduxx.com
www.paraduxx.com

OWNER: Duckhorn Wine Company.

LOCATION: 3 miles northeast of Yountville.

APPELLATIONS: Yountville, Napa Valley.

HOURS: 10 A.M.–4 P.M. daily.

TASTINGS: By appointment. Essential Tasting, $20 for 4 current releases and library wines; Enhanced Tasting, $30 for 5 limited-production wines. An Unpredictable Pair, $50 for tour and elaborate food-and-wine pairing, Thursday–Monday, 1 P.M. The Blend Experience, $40 for seated tasting of 3 core varietals and creating your own blend, Thursday–Sunday, 10:30 A.M. Howell Mountain Experience, $50 for tour of Howell Mountain and tasting of mountain vineyard wines, Friday–Sunday.

TOURS: By appointment with An Unpredictable Pair tasting.

THE WINES: Red blends of Cabernet Franc, Cabernet Sauvignon, Merlot, Petit Verdot, and Zinfandel; white blend of Chardonnay, Sauvignon Blanc, and Viognier.

SPECIALTIES: Zinfandel-based blends.

WINEMAKER: David Marchesi.

ANNUAL PRODUCTION: 20,000 cases.

OF SPECIAL NOTE: Gallery displays original paintings created for the winery's labels.

NEARBY ATTRACTIONS: Napa Valley Museum (winemaking displays, art exhibits).

PATZ & HALL

PATZ & HALL
851 Napa Valley Corporate
Way, Suite A
Napa, CA 94558
877-265-6700
info@patzhall.com
www.patzhall.com

OWNERS: Donald Patz,
Heather Patz, James Hall,
and Anne Moses.

LOCATION: 4 miles south of
downtown Napa.

APPELLATION: Napa Valley.

HOURS: 10 A.M.–4 P.M. daily
in summer, Wednesday–
Sunday in winter.

TASTINGS: $40 for 6
wines paired with food
complements by advance
reservation. $20 for 4
wines at Salon Bar
without reservation.

TOURS: None.

THE WINES: Chardonnay,
Pinot Noir.

SPECIALTY: Single-vineyard-
designated wines.

WINEMAKER: James Hall.

ANNUAL PRODUCTION:
26,000 cases.

OF SPECIAL NOTE: Patz &
Hall wines are available
for sale at the tasting
bar without advance
reservations during regular
operating hours.

NEARBY ATTRACTIONS:
Napa Valley Wine Train
(lunch, brunch, and
dinner excursions); Napa
Valley Opera House
(theatrical and musical
performances in historic
building).

The last place most people would think to look for a well-respected winery's tasting room would be in an anonymous complex of cookie-cutter office buildings. Granted, the exteriors are painted in a sophisticated palette of taupe and mauve. Only when the company's distinguished black and silver logo is close enough to see can visitors feel confident that they have arrived at the Patz & Hall Tasting Salon. The actual winemaking is done elsewhere, miles away on the east side of the town of Sonoma, where Patz & Hall established its own 30,000-square-foot winery in 2007 amid a fast-emerging neighborhood of similar facilities. Prior to that, Patz & Hall wines were produced at other Napa Valley wineries.

Patz & Hall was established in 1988, by four individuals—Donald Patz, James Hall, Anne Moses, and Heather Patz—who dedicated themselves to making benchmark wines sourced from distinctive California vineyards. Today, they produce a total of fifteen Chardonnays and Pinot Noirs, all without owning a single vine-yard themselves. Patz & Hall was founded on an unusual business model that began in the 1980s at Flora Springs Winery & Vineyards, when assistant winemaker James Hall and national sales manager Donald Patz forged a close friendship. Their mutual enthusiasm for wine produced from elite, small vineyards inspired them to blend their talents along with those of Anne Moses and Heather Patz. Together, the team boasted a wealth of knowledge and experience gleaned at such prestigious wineries as Far Niente, Girard Winery, and Honig Winery, where Hall was once the winemaker.

The founders apply their specialized expertise and daily attention to different areas of the family-run winery's operations. The cornerstone of Patz & Hall is this integrated, hands-on approach, combined with close personal relationships with growers who supply them with fruit from outstanding family-owned vineyards in Napa Valley, Russian River Valley, Mendocino County, Sonoma Coast, and Santa Lucia Highlands.

All along, the goal was to have a special place where they could welcome customers and get to know them in person. Opened in 2005 and freshly refurbished in 2008, the Patz & Hall Tasting Salon offers visitors two environments for wine and seasonal food pairings: the tasting bar that was added to the front room and a private salon beyond, where the bustle at most winery tasting rooms seems worlds away. In this secluded space, which is decorated like an exquisite dining room, guided tastings are held at a rectangular table made from reclaimed cherry wood and surrounded by eight chic straight-back chairs covered in a palomino shade of suede. Over the course of an hour or more, guests sample six wines paired with local farmstead cheeses and other light fare.

PEJU

S potting Peju, even on a winery-lined stretch of Highway 29, is easy, thanks to a fifty-foot-tall tasting tower topped with a distinctive copper roof. Although the tasting tower opened only in late 2003, the structure looks as if it has been there for decades. Like the rest of the property, it could have been transplanted directly from the countryside of southern France.

The Rutherford estate had been producing wine grapes for more than eighty years when Anthony and Herta Peju bought it in 1982. The couple has been improving the thirty-acre property ever since, streamlining vineyard techniques and adding Merlot and Cabernet Franc grapes to the estate's core product, Cabernet Sauvignon. By the mid-1990s, demand for Peju wines outstripped the winery's supply. To satisfy it, the Pejus acquired a 350-acre property in northern Napa County in the Pope Valley District, planted a variety of grapes, and named it Persephone Vineyard, after a goddess in Greek mythology.

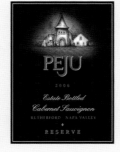

The Pejus entered the wine business by a somewhat circuitous route. Anthony Peju had been living in Europe when he was lured to Los Angeles by the movie industry, but then became interested in horticulture. After he met Herta Behensky, his future wife, he established his own nursery, yet secretly dreamed of owning a farm. The vibrant towns of Napa Valley and their proximity to San Francisco's cultural attractions enticed him to search for vineyard property. A two-year quest ended in the purchase of what would become Peju Province Winery.

Peju's horticultural experience, combined with his wife's talent for gardening, resulted in two acres of immaculately kept winery gardens. Together, they established a dramatic series of outdoor rooms linked by footpaths and punctuated with fountains and marble sculpture. Hundreds of flowering plants and trees create an aromatic retreat for the Pejus and their visitors. Lining both sides of the driveway are forty-foot-tall sycamore trees, their trunks adorned by gnarled spirals. Visitors reach the tasting room by crossing a small bridge over a pool with fountains. An entrance door of Brazilian cherrywood is carved with the image of a farm girl blending water and wine. Inside the room, three muses gaze down from a century-old stained-glass window. A copper-and-steel railing leads to the mezzanine, where a strategically placed circular window offers a garden view.

Peju remains a small, family-owned winery with two generations working together. Daughters Lisa and Ariana, who joined the family business, have been instrumental in installing solar panels at the winery (now a Napa Green Certified Winery), earning organic certification at Peju's Rutherford estate, and practicing sustainable farming at the winery's other two properties.

PEJU
8466 St. Helena Hwy.
(Hwy. 29)
Rutherford, CA 94573
707-963-3600
800-446-7358
info@peju.com
www.peju.com

OWNERS: Anthony and Herta Peju.

LOCATION: 11 miles north of the town of Napa.

APPELLATIONS: Rutherford, Napa Valley.

HOURS: 10 A.M.–6 P.M. daily.

TASTINGS: $15.

TOURS: Self-guided or by appointment.

THE WINES: Cabernet Franc, Cabernet Sauvignon, Chardonnay, Merlot, Provence, Sauvignon Blanc, Syrah, Zinfandel.

SPECIALTIES: Reserve Cabernet Sauvignon, H.B. Vineyard Cabernet Sauvignon, Fifty/fifty (red wine).

WINEMAKER: Sara Fowler.

ANNUAL PRODUCTION: 35,000 cases.

OF SPECIAL NOTE: Wine-and-food pairings, cooking classes, gift boutique. Approximately 80 percent of wines available only at winery.

NEARBY ATTRACTIONS: Silverado Museum (Robert Louis Stevenson memorabilia); Napa Valley Museum (winemaking displays, art exhibits); Culinary Institute of America at Greystone (cooking demonstrations).

PINE RIDGE VINEYARDS

PINE RIDGE VINEYARDS
5901 Silverado Trail
Napa, CA 94558
707-252-9777
800-575-9777
concierge@pineridgewine.
com
www.pineridgevineyards.
com

OWNER: Crimson Wine Group.

LOCATION: 4 miles southeast of Yountville.

APPELLATION: Stags Leap District.

HOURS: 10:30 A.M.–4:30 P.M. daily.

TASTINGS: $15 for 5 wines; $25 for 5 reserve wines.

TOURS: By appointment. 10 A.M., 12 P.M., and 2 P.M. daily.

THE WINES: Cabernet Sauvignon, Chardonnay, Chenin Blanc, Malbec, Merlot, Petit Verdot, Viognier.

SPECIALTIES: Appellation Cabernet Sauvignons, red Bordeaux blends, Fortis multi-appellation Cabernet Sauvignon.

WINEMAKER: Michael Beaulac.

ANNUAL PRODUCTION: 40,000.

OF SPECIAL NOTE: Food-and-wine pairing seminars with lunch on Sundays at 11 a.m. ($65); reservations required.

NEARBY ATTRACTION: Napa Valley Museum (winemaking displays, art exhibits), Napa Valley Opera House (live performances in historic building).

On the heels of the 1976 Paris tasting that rocked the wine world, Gary and Nancy Andrus founded Pine Ridge Vineyards. Just two years after French judges declared a Silverado Trail Cabernet Sauvignon superior to its French competitors, the couple bought property in the suddenly famous Stags Leap region and began producing wine in an old farmhouse. Gary, a former Olympic skier, mastered the art of winemaking, while Nancy handled sales.

The Andruses focused on classic Bordeaux-style reds and Chardonnay. They championed innovation among area vintners by encouraging tight vine spacing to control plant vigor and concentrate varietal flavors, implementing gravity flow in the cellar as a means of handling the wine more gently, and, in 1983, hiring a female winemaker. In the 1990s, the winery became the first in California to blend Viognier with Chenin Blanc to produce a delightfully fresh and floral wine that remains an unusual offering.

Tucked among oak-and-pine-clad hills, the winery's simple architecture reflects its farmhouse beginnings. Multicolored Joseph's Coat roses greet visitors at the gate, and the short driveway passes between clipped lawns, shade trees, and pocket gardens offering restful seating with panoramic views of the estate's vineyards. A rough-hewn pergola shelters a plaque describing the varied trellising systems displayed in the adjacent demonstration vineyard. Opposite the winery grows one of the few Chardonnay vineyards in the Stags Leap District. Here, seasonal fog settles briefly each day to cool slopes that would otherwise be too hot for the Burgundian grape, fostering fruit with wonderfully balanced components. A hand-stacked rock wall and matching arch mark the boundary of the nearly two-acre block, dubbed Le Petit Clos ("the little enclosure"). In total, the winery boasts 200 acres of estate vineyards spanning five Napa Valley appellations (Carneros, Howell Mountain, Oakville, Rutherford, and Stags Leap), with 45 acres in the coveted Stags Leap District.

The tasting room's french doors open onto a carpeted salon with muted colors, partial walls of stone, and a tasting bar of dark Honduran mahogany and polished black granite along two sides. Through a glass wall fitted with transparent doors, visitors can see into the original barrel room, a softly lit gallery where liquid beauties sleep. An additional 4,600 French oak barrels rest in the winery's caves, excavated from solid rock over a period of twenty years. The caves comprise nearly a mile of underground tunnels. At the end of one wide chamber, cool air, low light, and a display of art glass resembling luminous sea creatures amplify the spirit of a moist, mysterious grotto.

PROVENANCE VINEYARDS

Provenance Vineyards takes its name from a French noun referring to origins and authenticity. True to the spirit of its name, the winery sources fruit from acclaimed Napa Valley vineyards, including legendary plantings in the Rutherford appellation. Lauded as the valley's "sweet spot" for Cabernet Sauvignon, the appellation stretches from Yountville to St. Helena. Its location at the widest, sunniest part of the valley, combined with its alluvial soil—dubbed "Rutherford dust" by famed enologist André Tchelistcheff—results in an exceptional *terroir* that produces complex Cabernet Sauvignon with uniquely expressed qualities of berry and spice.

For its flagship wine, Provenance Vineyards purchases Cabernet Sauvignon from Rutherford's renowned Beckstoffer Vineyard Rancho Caymus. The old rancho by George Yount, who came is widely regarded as the first in the valley. When Yount's Thomas Rutherford in 1864, he acres that would become the

George III, originally part of was a Mexican land grant owned to Napa Valley in 1838 and person to plant wine grapes granddaughter married vintner gave the couple about a thousand heart of the Rutherford region. In 1928 Georges de Latour, founder of Beaulieu Vineyard, acquired the vineyard, christening it BV No. 3. By 1988 respected grower Andy Beckstoffer had purchased the vineyard and begun replanting with vines better suited to local conditions. Beckstoffer bought four adjacent parcels and renamed the now 300-acre property in honor of wine pioneer Georges de Latour.

The winery also sources Cabernet Sauvignon, as well as Cabernet Franc, from Beckstoffer's To Kalon Vineyard, located in the Oakville appellation three miles south of Rutherford. First planted to wine grapes in 1868, it was replanted in the mid-1990s with a variety of improved clones.

Tom Rinaldi, director of winemaking and Provenance's founding winemaker, was also the founding winemaker at Duckhorn Vineyards, where he spent twenty-two years working with Napa Valley Merlot and Cabernet Sauvignon. Among his most celebrated Merlot providers was Three Palms Vineyard. He and winemaker Chris Cooney continue to purchase Merlot, along with small amounts of other varieties for blending, from this prestigious vineyard.

An eye-catching landmark along Highway 29, the burgundy-red winery is surrounded by the estate vineyard, planted to twelve acres of Sauvignon Blanc and Semillon. The boutique tasting room features a distinctive floor handcrafted from nine hundred of the winery's barrels, complete with cooperage brands. Behind the elegant horseshoe-shaped tasting bar is a round, six-foot window that offers tasters a tantalizing peek into the winery.

PROVENANCE VINEYARDS
1695 St. Helena Hwy.
Rutherford, CA 94573
707-968-3633
866-946-3252
provenance.info@
provenancevineyards.com
www.provenance
vineyards.com

OWNER: Diageo Chateau and Estate Wines.

LOCATION: About 3 miles south of St. Helena.

APPELLATION: Rutherford.

HOURS: 10:30 A.M.–5:30 P.M. daily.

TASTINGS: $20 for any 4 wines.

TOURS: None.

THE WINES: Cabernet Sauvignon, Merlot, Sauvignon Blanc.

SPECIALTY: Rutherford Cabernet Sauvignon.

WINEMAKER: Chris Cooney.

ANNUAL PRODUCTION: 45,000 cases.

OF SPECIAL NOTE: Las Amigas Merlot, Cabernet Franc, Malbec, Estate Sauvignon Blanc, and Winemakers Reserve Blend (red Bordeaux blend) available in tasting room only.

NEARBY ATTRACTIONS: Culinary Institute of America at Greystone (cooking demonstrations); Bothe-Napa State Park (hiking, picnicking, horseback riding, swimming Memorial Day–Labor Day); Bale Grist Mill State Historic Park (water-powered mill circa 1846); Silverado Museum (Robert Louis Stevenson memorabilia).

ROBERT MONDAVI WINERY

ROBERT MONDAVI WINERY
7801 Hwy. 29
Oakville, CA 94562
707-968-2000
888-766-6328
info@robertmondavi
winery.com
www.robertmondavi.com

LOCATION: About 10 miles north of the town of Napa.

APPELLATIONS: Oakville, Napa Valley.

HOURS: 10 A.M.–5 P.M. daily.

TASTINGS: $20 for 4 wines in main tasting room; $30 for 4 wines or by the glass in To Kalon tasting room.

TOURS: Signature tour every hour by reservation ($25); other tours available seasonally.

THE WINES: Cabernet Sauvignon, Chardonnay, Fumé Blanc, Merlot, Moscato D'Oro, Pinot Noir.

SPECIALTIES: Cabernet Sauvignon Reserve and Fumé Blanc Reserve.

WINEMAKER: Genevieve Janssens.

ANNUAL PRODUCTION: 300,000 cases.

OF SPECIAL NOTE: Guided educational tastings and food-and-wine pairings. Large shop with wine books and Italian imports. Summer Festival Concert Series (July); Cabernet Sauvignon Reserve Release Party (September).

NEARBY ATTRACTIONS: Culinary Institute of America at Greystone (cooking demonstrations); Napa Valley Museum (winemaking displays, art exhibits).

Wineries come and wineries go in Napa Valley, but in this fast-paced, high-stakes world, few can challenge the lasting achievements of the Robert Mondavi Winery. Since its inception more than forty years ago, it has remained in the forefront of innovation, from the use of cold fermentation, stainless steel tanks, and small French oak barrels to the collaboration with NASA employing aerial imaging to reveal the health and vigor of grapevines.

Founder Robert Mondavi's cherished goal of producing wines on a par with the best in the world made his name virtually synonymous with California winemaking. That vision is being carried out today with ambitious programs such as the To Kalon Project. Named after the historic estate vineyard surrounding the winery, this extensive renovation led to the unveiling of the To Kalon Fermentation Cellar, which capitalizes on the natural flow of gravity to transport wine through the production system. Although Robert Mondavi pioneered the use of stainless steel fermentation in the 1960s, To Kalon has returned to traditional oak fermentation, based on the belief that the use of oak enhances the aromas, flavors,

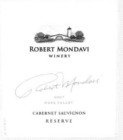

and complexity of the winery's reserve, district, and vineyard-designated Cabernet Sauvignon.

Technological advances aside, the best reason for visiting Robert Mondavi Winery is something less tangible: an opportunity to experience the presentation of wine in the broader context of lifestyle. Educational tours and tastings, concerts, art exhibits, and the industry's first culinary program are all part of the Mondavi legacy. One of the most popular offerings is the Signature tour and tasting, which follows the path of the grape from the vine through the cellar to the finished wine. The 550-acre vineyard was named To Kalon (Greek for "the beautiful") by Hamilton Walker Crabb, a winegrowing pioneer who established vineyards here in the late 1800s. It was this property that inspired Robert Mondavi to establish his winery on the site.

Just as the estate's grapes express their *terroir*, the winery itself reflects the location and legacy of Napa Valley. The Spanish mission-style architecture, with its expansive archway and bell tower designed by Clifford May, pays homage to the Franciscan fathers who planted the first grapes in the region. Two long wings project from the open-air lobby to embrace a wide expanse of lawn framed by the Mayacamas Range on the western horizon. Typical of the winery's commitment to the arts, several sculptures by regional artist Beniamino Benvenuto Bufano (who, like Robert Mondavi's family, came from Italy) are displayed in the courtyard and elsewhere around the grounds. In addition, the winery features art exhibits that change every two months.

ROMBAUER VINEYARDS

The quarter-mile-long drive from the Silverado Trail leads to a winery ensconced in a forest of pine trees. On the far side of the low-slung building, a wide California ranch–style porch affords views that extend to the tree-covered ridge of the Mayacamas Range to the southeast. Without another structure in sight, the serene setting has the ambience of a fairy-tale kingdom secluded from the hustle and bustle of the valley floor. Directly below the winery, a gravel path winds down to a hill where roses are planted in the sun and azaleas thrive in the shade. Scattered about are a half-dozen metal sculptures of fantastical creatures such as a diminutive dinosaur and a life-size winged horse, all weathered to the point that they blend into the landscape.

The Rombauer family traces its heritage to another fertile wine area, the Rheingau region in Germany, where Koerner Rombauer's ancestors made wine. His great-aunt Irma Rombauer wrote the classic book *The Joy of Cooking*. The tradition of linking wine to food is carried on today, with every member of the family involved in the daily operation of the winery, from selecting grapes to marketing the final product. K. R. (Koerner Rombauer III) and his sister, Sheana, are now in charge, respectively, of national sales and public relations.

Koerner Rombauer, a former commercial airline captain, and his late wife, Joan, met and married in Southern California, where both had grown up in an agricultural environment. Since they had always wanted their children to have rural childhood experiences similar to their own, they came to the Napa Valley in search of land. In 1972 they bought fifty acres and settled into a home just up the hill from where the winery sits today. Within a few years, they became partners in a nearby winery. Their hands-on involvement in the winery's operations whetted their appetite for a label of their own and for making handcrafted wines with the passion and commitment of the family tradition. Taking advantage of the topography, the Rombauers built their family winery into the side of the hill. Rombauer Vineyards was completed in 1982.

By the early 1990s, the Rombauers realized they had the perfect location for excavating wine storage caves. Completed in 1997, the double-horseshoe-shaped cellar extends for more than a mile into the hillside. Tours begin in the tasting room, which is personalized with an eclectic assortment of memorabilia from Koerner Rombauer's life. Among the more interesting items are the many signed photographs of famous people as diverse as test pilot Chuck Yeager, entertainer Barbra Streisand, former Secretary of State George Shultz, and country music star Garth Brooks, many of them with personal notes to Rombauer.

ROMBAUER VINEYARDS
3522 Silverado Trail
St. Helena, CA 94574
800-622-2206
707-963-5170
www.rombauer.com

OWNER:
Koerner Rombauer.

LOCATION: 1.5 miles north of Deer Park Rd.

APPELLATION: Napa Valley.

HOURS: 10 A.M.–5 P.M. daily.

TASTINGS: By appointment. $10.

TOURS: By appointment.

THE WINES: Cabernet Sauvignon, Chardonnay, Merlot, Zinfandel.

SPECIALTY: Diamond Selection Cabernet Sauvignon.

WINEMAKER: Richie Allen.

ANNUAL PRODUCTION: 68,000 cases.

OF SPECIAL NOTE: Tours include visit to barrel-aging cellar. Copies of the latest edition of *The Joy of Cooking* and other cookbooks by Irma Rombauer are available in the tasting room. Zinfandel Port and Joy, a late-harvest Chardonnay, available only at winery.

NEARBY ATTRACTIONS: Bothe-Napa State Park (hiking, picnicking, horse-back riding, swimming Memorial Day–Labor Day); Silverado Museum (Robert Louis Stevenson memorabilia); Culinary Institute of America at Greystone (cooking demonstrations).

RUBICON ESTATE

RUBICON ESTATE
1991 St. Helena Hwy.
Rutherford, CA 94573
707-968-1100
800-RUBICON
reservations@rubiconestate.
com
www.rubiconestate.com

OWNERS: Francis and
Eleanor Coppola.

LOCATION: About 3 miles
south of St. Helena.

APPELLATIONS: Rutherford,
Napa Valley.

HOURS: 10 A.M.–5 P.M. daily.

TASTINGS: $25 guest fee
includes tasting of 5 estate
wines.

TOURS: Daily (707-968-1161
for reservations and fees).

THE WINES: Blancaneaux
(white blend), Cask
Cabernet Sauvignon, Estate
Merlot, Pennino Zinfandel,
RC Reserve Syrah, Rubicon
(red blend).

SPECIALTY: Rubicon.

WINEMAKER: Scott McLeod.

ANNUAL PRODUCTION:
Unavailable.

OF SPECIAL NOTE: Historic
wine and magic lantern
museum. Extensive shop
with estate olive oil, books,
wine accessories, and
gifts. More than 200 acres
of organically certified
vineyards. Tableside tastings
offered at Mammarella's
Wine Bar.

NEARBY ATTRACTIONS:
Silverado Museum
(Robert Louis Stevenson
memorabilia); Napa Valley
Museum (winemaking
displays, art exhibits);
Culinary Institute of
America at Greystone
(cooking demonstrations).

Academy Award–winning filmmaker Francis Ford Coppola and his wife, Eleanor, started making wine at the old Niebaum estate in 1975. Twenty years later, they bought the winery as well as the nineteenth-century château and adjacent vineyards. Flash back to 1879, when Gustave Niebaum, a Finnish sea captain, invested the fortune he acquired in the Alaska fur trade to establish his own winery, Inglenook. He modeled the massive stone château on the estates he had visited in Bordeaux. By the time the Coppolas entered the picture, however, a series of corporate ownerships had left the estate bereft of its reputation, its label, and much of its vineyard land.

The Coppolas reunited the major parcels of the original estate, which they named Niebaum-Coppola, and began restoring and renovating the château and its grounds to their former glory. The European-style front courtyard now graced with grapevines. Nearby, a is illuminated at night. In the vaulted most dramatic creations, a grand imported from Belize. The Coppolas milestones in Inglenook's long,

features a redwood and stone pergola ninety-by-thirty-foot reflecting pool entrance is one of Francis Coppola's staircase built of exotic hardwoods also mounted exhibits celebrating illustrious history.

When Francis Coppola set out the acclaimed estate vineyards, he to craft a proprietary red wine using found "the crossing of the Rubicon," Caesar's march on Rome, to be an appropriate metaphor in its implied "point of no return." So it was fitting that he renamed the winery Rubicon Estate in 2006, when the winery introduced profound changes to its image in general and its visitor programs in particular. In the past, thousands of people simply dropped in and wandered around the estate on their own, maybe staying for a tasting or to browse the extraordinary gift shop. To offer a more streamlined, personalized experience, the Coppolas decided to increase the emphasis on wine and education. To that end, visitors are charged a guest fee, good for three days, that entitles them to access to the château and Centennial Museum, and a tasting of five estate wines.

Visitors seeking a more in-depth experience of Rubicon Estate and its winemaking may sign up for any of several educational tours: Sensory, an exploration of the flavors and aromas of selected wines; Elevage, an extensive enological tour covering the various steps in the production of wine and including a visit to the underground caves and a barrel sample; Vinifera, a guided walk in the estate vineyard to learn about the special qualities of the Rutherford appellation; Janus, a food-and-wine pairing with specialties prepared by the winery chef, offered seasonally; and personalized private tours. Most of these tours include wine tasting.

Welcome to
RUTHERFORD
HILL

A TERLATO FAMILY PROPERTY

RUTHERFORD HILL WINERY

East of the Silverado Trail, a winding mountain road leads to one of Napa Valley's legendary wineries. Here, visitors will find Rutherford Hill Winery, tucked into a hillside and offering a stunning view of the valley. With its gambrel roof and rough-hewn redwood timbers, the winery resembles an antique barn. The building is large enough to house both the winery and the inviting tasting room with its relaxed atmosphere. At the entrance is a massive redwood trellis that shades the courtyard and the gigantic doors leading to the tasting room. The winery is framed by expansive lawns and gardens, and a picnic area set in Napa Valley's oldest olive grove.

Rutherford Hill also possesses one of the largest wine-aging cave systems in North America. Begun in 1982 and completed by 1990, the caves are nearly a mile in length. They maintain a natural temperature of fifty-nine degrees Fahrenheit and a relative humidity of 80 percent, conditions that provide the perfect environment and ecologically sensitive way to protect and age the wines. Entering the caves through large doors flanked by towering cypress and grapevines, visitors immediately notice the heady perfumes of oak and aging Merlot and Cabernet.

Rutherford Hill Winery was built in 1972 by Joseph Phelps, who soon went on to establish another winery in his own name. In 1976 Bill and Lila Jaeger bought the hilltop property, noting that the region's soils resembled those of Pomerol, a Bordeaux appellation famed for its outstanding Merlot-based wines. The local loam, or "Rutherford dust," a term coined in the late 1930s by famed Russian enologist André Tchelistcheff, is credited with imparting great depth and flavor to the area's plantings of Merlot and Cabernet Sauvignon.

In 1996 Anthony Terlato, a well-known figure in the American fine wine industry, acquired Rutherford Hill with the single-minded goal of producing the finest wines in the Rutherford appellation. Terlato had started his career in his father's Chicago retail wine shop in the 1950s and parlayed a modest business into a leading importer of fine wines. Shortly after purchasing Rutherford Hill, he built a state-of-the-art winery where the winemaker could separately vinify grapes coming from different vineyard lots and grown in many different and idiosyncratic soil types. This allowed the Terlatos and the winemaking team to focus on the specific vineyards producing the finest grapes, which are now the foundation of Rutherford Hill wines. Today, Merlot makes up most of the winery's production, underscoring the enduring appeal of wines grown in the renowned Rutherford dust.

RUTHERFORD HILL WINERY
200 Rutherford Hill Rd.
Rutherford, CA 94573
1-800-MERLOT1
707-963-1871
info@rutherfordhill.com
www.rutherfordhill.com

OWNERS: Terlato family.

LOCATION: About 2 miles south of St. Helena, just north of Rutherford Cross Rd. east of Silverado Trail.

APPELLATION: Rutherford.

HOURS: 10 A.M.–5 P.M. daily.

TASTINGS: $15 for 4 wines, $20 for 6 wines, $25 for 6 reserve wines.

TOURS: Cave and winery tour and tasting ($20), daily at 11:30 A.M., 1:30 P.M., and 3:30 P.M. Reservations preferred.

THE WINES: Cabernet Franc, Cabernet Sauvignon, Chardonnay, Malbec, Merlot, Port, Sangiovese, Sauvignon Blanc.

SPECIALTIES: Merlot, Bordeaux blends.

WINEMAKER: Marisa Taylor Huffaker.

ANNUAL PRODUCTION: 50,000 cases.

OF SPECIAL NOTE: Blend Your Own Merlot program ($95), Saturdays at 11 A.M., is held in wine cave and includes winery tour and tasting. Passport weekends in November and May. Gift shop features items such as crystal stemware and wine accessories. Winery is pet friendly. Reserve and limited-release wines available only in tasting room. Picnic area.

NEARBY ATTRACTIONS: Culinary Institute of America at Greystone (cooking demonstrations); Silverado Museum (Robert Louis Stevenson memorabilia).

SADDLEBACK CELLARS

SADDLEBACK CELLARS
7802 Money Rd.
Oakville CA 94562
707-944-1305
tastingroom@
saddlebackcellars.com
www.saddlebackcellars.com

OWNERS: Venge family.

LOCATION: 1 mile east of Oakville.

APPELLATION: Oakville.

HOURS: 10 A.M.–4 P.M. daily.

TASTINGS: : By appointment. $20 for 7 wines.

TOURS: None.

THE WINES: Cabernet Sauvignon, Chardonnay, Merlot, Pinot Blanc, Pinot Grigio, Syrah, Viognier, Zinfandel.

SPECIALTIES: Cabernet Sauvignon, Merlot, Zinfandel.

WINEMAKER: Nils Venge.

ANNUAL PRODUCTION: 6,000 cases.

OF SPECIAL NOTE: Tag Along party, including wine, live country rock music, and barbecue, held twice a year in January/February and July/August. Winery is pet friendly.

NEARBY ATTRACTION: Napa Valley Museum (winemaking displays, art exhibits).

Turning into Saddleback Cellars, past the basketball hoop and mailbox mounted on an old produce scale, tasters may feel as if they're visiting a friend's country bungalow. A lone wagon wheel rests against the concrete block winery, and Old Glory waves below weathered wooden gables. Grapevines border the driveway, which doubles as a crush pad during harvest, and clustered farm and winery equipment attest to the property's utilitarian purpose.

Owner/winemaker Nils Venge parks his 1940s-era Ford tractors near the winery and often can be seen riding high among the vines of his fifteen-acre vineyard. He makes wine using his estate Cabernet Sauvignon, Merlot, Chardonnay, and Pinot Blanc varieties, as well as fruit sourced from select Northern California vine-yards. Venge also owns Envy Wines, with partner Mark Carter, in nearby Calistoga, and Cougar's Leap, in Lake County, and he consults for several others.

An energetic Dane with a ready smile, Venge grew up in Southern California. He mastered cowboy skills at an early age and even rode his horse in the Pasadena Rose Parade. As a youth, he worked in his father's wholesale wine business, then earned degrees in viticulture and enology at U.C. Davis. In 1970 he managed the vineyards at Charles Krug Winery, before moving to Sterling Vineyards in 1972. Venge became Villa Mt. Eden's first winemaker in 1973 and produced a series of prized Cabernet Sauvignon. Three years later, he purchased the property that would become Saddleback Cellars and replanted the estate vineyard. He pressed his label's first vintage in 1982. Venge was appointed Groth Winery's inaugural winemaker in 1982 and made headlines by crafting the winery's 1985 Reserve Cabernet Sauvignon, the first American wine to receive one hundred points from Robert Parker Jr. of *The Wine Advocate*. Venge celebrated Saddleback Cellars' twenty-fifth anniversary in 2006 by bottling a commemorative Cabernet Sauvignon. On the label is a photo of a grinning Venge at six years old, riding high on a bucking bronco.

In the picnic area opposite the winery, visitors can share a little cowboy magic by taking snapshots with the "photo pony"—a western saddle cinched to a barrel with a rope tail. Sycamore trees shade redwood tables nearby, where guests can enjoy alfresco tastings of the wines. Tastings also take place in the barrel room, a warren of barrel racks, stacked cases, and wooden gift boxes festooned with award ribbons and knotted bandanas. Leather-topped stools afford seating at a table made from an antique redwood fermenter, as country-western tunes twang softly in the background.

SILVER OAK CELLARS

Fans of fine Cabernet Sauvignon line up hours in advance—sometimes even camping overnight—for the new release of each Silver Oak wine. The vigil has become something of a ritual for connoisseurs who want to be sure to take home some of the winery's hard-to-find bottles. During the early 1990s, on each semiannual Silver Oak Release Day in Napa Valley, just a handful of people waited for the winery doors to open, but as news of the extraordinary wine spread and the crowds grew larger, Silver  Oak Cellars began serving espresso drinks and doughnuts to the early-morning crowds and passing hot hors d'oeuvres throughout the after-noon. Now many wine lovers from all over the country plan vacations around the festive events, which are always held the first Saturday in February and August.

The biggest attraction is what lies in the bottle. Silver Oak produces elegant Cabernet Sauvignons with fully developed flavors and seamless textures. The winemaking program combines meticulous vineyard practices, harmonious blending, and extensive aging in exclusively American oak barrels—followed by even further aging in bottles. By the time the wine reaches the consumer, it is a synergy of depth and delicacy.

The success of Silver Oak Cellars began with two visionary men, Ray Duncan and Justin Meyer. Duncan was an entrepreneur in Colorado before being lured to California in the 1960s. Impressed with the potential for wines in Napa Valley and Alexander Valley in Sonoma County, he purchased 750 acres of pastures, orchards, and vineyards within a year. In 1972 he formed a partnership with Meyer, a former Christian Brothers winemaker. The partners' work together lasted thirty years, until Meyer passed away in 2002.

Today the Duncan family sustains the commitment to excellence that has long been a hallmark of Silver Oak Cellars, which has a sister estate in Geyserville in Sonoma County's Alexander Valley. Each estate is devoted to an individual style of Cabernet Sauvignon. The Alexander Valley wine has a particularly soft and fruity character, while the somewhat bolder Napa Valley wine has firmer tannins, making it appropriate for longer cellar aging. The historic dairy barn that housed the original Napa winery burned in 2006 and was replaced by a new building faced with reclaimed limestone from an abandoned flour mill. Opened in time to crush the 2008 vintage, the Oakville facility has a hospitality center and timber-framed tasting room. The room is enhanced with two stained-glass windows from the original facility and a pair of new ones by the same artist. A custom glass wine cellar displays Silver Oak's vintages from 1972 to the present.

SILVER OAK CELLARS
915 Oakville Cross Rd.
Oakville, CA 94562
707-944-8808
800-273-8809
info@silveroak.com
www.silveroak.com

OWNERS: Duncan family.

LOCATION: 1.2 miles east of Hwy 29.

APPELLATIONS: Napa Valley, Alexander Valley.

HOURS: 9 A.M.–5 P.M. Monday–Saturday, 11 A.M.–5 P.M. Sunday, in summer; 9 A.M.–4 P.M. Monday–Saturday, 11 A.M.–4 P.M. Sunday, in winter.

TASTINGS: $20 (complimentary glass included). Reservations suggested for groups of 8 or more.

TOURS: Monday–Saturday, 10 A.M. and 1 P.M.; Food pairing, Monday–Thursday, 2 P.M.

THE WINE: Cabernet Sauvignon.

SPECIALTY: Cabernet Sauvignon.

WINEMAKER: Daniel Baron.

ANNUAL PRODUCTION: 30,000 cases.

OF SPECIAL NOTE: Release Day is held simultaneously at both estates for each wine: Napa Valley Cabernet on the first Saturday in February; Alexander Valley Cabernet on the first Saturday in August. Purchase limits on some vintages.

NEARBY ATTRACTION: Napa Valley Museum (winemaking displays, art exhibits).

SOMERSTON WINE CO.

SOMERSTON WINE CO.
6490 Washington St.
Yountville, CA 94599
707-944-8200
visit@somerstonwineco.com
www.somerstonwineco.com

OWNERS: Allan Chapman, John Wilson, Craig Becker.

LOCATION: Tasting Lounge is in downtown Yountville.

APPELLATION: Napa Valley.

HOURS: 10 A.M.–10 P.M. Tuesday–Saturday; 10 A.M.–8 P.M. Sunday and Monday.

TASTINGS: $10 for 3 wines, $20 for 5 wines.

TOURS: $50 for 2-hour tour of Somerston, winery, and vineyards. By appointment.

THE WINES: Cabernet Sauvignon, Grenache, Grenache Blanc, Malbec, Merlot, Petite Sirah, Petit Verdot, Sauvignon Blanc, Semillon, Syrah, Viognier, Zinfandel.

SPECIALTIES: Cabernet Sauvignon, Grenache Blanc, Merlot, Petite Sirah, Sauvignon Blanc, Syrah.

WINEMAKER: Craig Becker.

ANNUAL PRODUCTION: 8,500 cases.

OF SPECIAL NOTE: Food-pairing seminars and classes pairing gardening with wine offered weekly by reservation. Live music and movies on summer nights. Somerston occasionally offers on-site cooking classes and gardening workshops followed by lunch paired with wine. Reservations required.

NEARBY ATTRACTION: Napa Valley Museum (winemaking displays, art exhibits).

Opened in 2010 and suggesting a small Tuscan villa, Somerston's retail complex in downtown Yountville features stone lintels, exposed patches of locally quarried rock, and wooden shutters flanking the second-story windows. Across an adjacent courtyard, the winery's retail market stocks farm-fresh goods, including local cheeses, deli items, meats, and produce, some of it grown on the Somerston ranch, located about fifteen miles northeast of Yountville. The winery bottles fourteen different wines under three labels: Somerston, Priest Ranch, and Highflyer. The last was introduced by co-owner and winemaker Craig Becker, a private pilot who made wine at Spring Mountain Vineyard for seven years.

Inside the wine-tasting lounge, beside two slab-cut walnut tasting cabinetry all were fashioned from the winery's 1,628-acre ranch. With an eighteen-foot-wide photographic grazing at Somerston on display, the

In addition to wine tasting in an offers visitors a rare opportunity to

visitors sit on soft sofas or in tall chairs bars. The rich brown bars, floor, and fallen walnut trees that once grew on oil paintings, metal sculptures, and mural of estate vineyards and sheep space doubles as a casual art gallery. elegant storefront setting, the winery explore a working ranch. Arranged by advance appointment only, winery and vineyard tours of Somerston are conducted in the open-air comfort of an ATV buggy, and cover a good portion of this part of Napa Valley's rural paradise. A wonderland of native oaks, natural springs, and wildlife, the property includes several acres dedicated to gardens, a lake with an island gazebo, and 1,500 head of Dorper sheep. The more than two hundred acres of sustainably farmed vineyards range in elevation from 850 to 2,400 feet above sea level. They are planted to eleven different grape varieties and supply 65 percent of the fruit required for the winery's production.

Located on the ranch inside a renovated, 12,000-square-foot barn, the winemaking facility has a carbon-neutral cooling, heating, and hot water system. An adjacent tasting room has a polished concrete floor, paneling salvaged from an old redwood barn, and soft chairs for seated tastings. Nearby is an insectary that provides beneficial insects for vineyard health, and a second barn for special events.

This ambitious project took shape in 2004, when co-owner F. Allan Chapman bought the 638-acre Priest Ranch. The historical name of the property paid tribute to the first person to settle the land, in 1849. In 2005 Chapman added a neighboring, 990-acre stretch of rolling hills and meadows that included vineyards planted between 1970 and 1999.

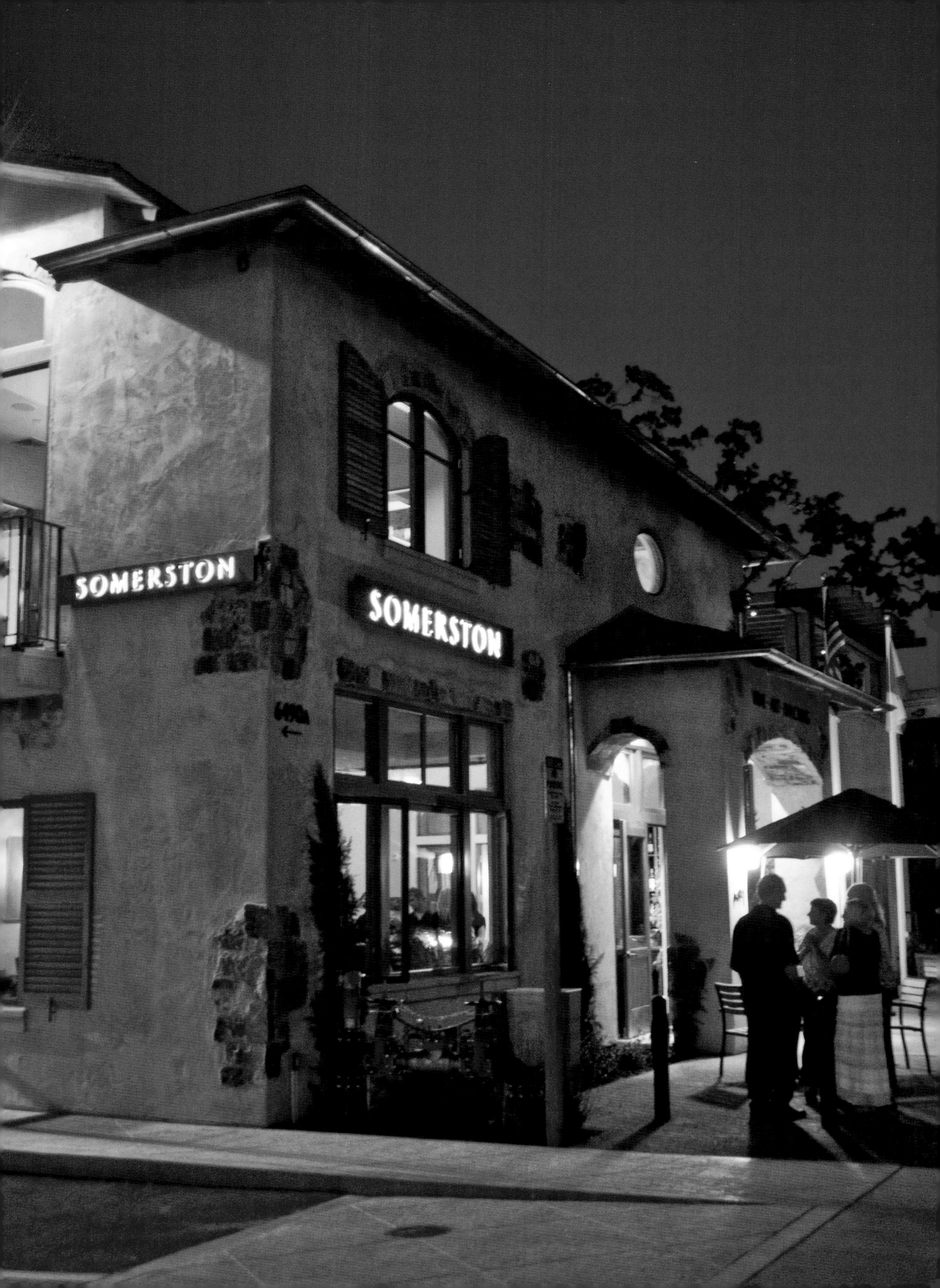
SOMERSTON
SOMERSTON

SPRING MOUNTAIN VINEYARD

When visitors arrive at Spring Mountain Vineyard, time seems to slow. Weathered stones reinforce vineyard terraces, a glass greenhouse sparkles in the distance, and gnarled olive trees attest to more than a century of cultivation. As early as 1873, European immigrants planted wine grapes in the Spring Mountain region. In 1885 Mexican-born Tiburcio Parrott began clearing the 800 acres that one day would mark the heart of Spring Mountain Vineyard. Parrott built a three-story Victorian home on a rise overlooking St. Helena and named it Miravalle ("valley view"). He planted olive orchards and 120 acres of grapes, and also tunneled into a hillside to make storage for 4,000  gallons of wine. In 1894 Parrott's Cabernet Sauvignon won first place at the San Francisco Mid Winter Fair, but after his death that same year, the estate was closed.

Over the next hundred years, the Parrott estate changed hands, each owner making his personal mark. In 1974, a 17,000-square-foot winery was built in a style blending Queen Anne elements with European-style architecture. Fitting snugly against the hillside that harbors the caves, the winery features dormers along a mansard roof, and a tower and curved cupola. The winery was then named Spring Mountain for its wealth of natural springs and the steepness of the terrain.

In 1992 Spring Mountain Vineyard was purchased by its current owner, who subsequently acquired three more historic estates—Chateau Chevalier (also dating back to the 1800s), Streblow Vineyards, and Draper Vineyards—creating one of the largest and oldest contiguous wine estates in Napa Valley. The 227 acres of vineyards range from 400 to 1,600 feet in elevation and provide a variety of sustainably farmed fruit with such mountain-grown qualities as intense color, concentrated flavors, and enhanced aging potential. By 2000 the winery excavated a 22,000-square-foot cave network designed to connect with Parrott's original tunnel. The two caves are filled with pristine French oak barrels in which the estate wines age before bottling.

Elaborate seated wine tastings are conducted in the cave at a massive table made from windfall redwood or in the Victorian mansion beneath the illumination of crystal chandeliers. More informal tastings are held in the charming yellow Spring House, a former caretaker's cottage built in the 1940s. Outside the cottage, amid olive trees and facing a view of terraced vineyards, guests may relax in Adirondack chairs with a glass of estate-bottled wine.

SPRING MOUNTAIN VINEYARD
2805 Spring Mountain Rd.
St. Helena, CA 94574
707-967-4188
877-769-4637
reserve@springmtn.com
www.springmountain
vineyard.com

OWNER: Jacob E. Safra.

LOCATION: 1.5 miles northwest of downtown St. Helena.

APPELLATIONS: Napa Valley, Spring Mountain District.

HOURS: 10 A.M.–4 P.M. daily.

TASTINGS: By appointment. First Tier Tasting, $25 including 1 library wine; Estate Tasting, $35 for seated tasting of current releases and 1 library wine; Library Tasting, $50 for Cabernet Sauvignon or Elivette vertical.

TOURS: Estate Tastings include tour of winery, extensive caves, and historic grounds.

THE WINES: Cabernet Sauvignon, Chardonnay, Pinot Noir, Sauvignon Blanc, Syrah.

SPECIALTIES: Elivette and Bordeaux-style blends, estate-bottled wines.

WINEMAKER: Jac Cole.

ANNUAL PRODUCTION: 8,000 cases.

OF SPECIAL NOTE: Winery features historic architecture and extensive caves.

NEARBY ATTRACTIONS: Culinary Institute of America (cooking demonstrations); Bothe-Napa State Park (hiking, picnicking, horseback riding, swimming Memorial Day–Labor Day); Silverado Museum (Robert Louis Stevenson memorabilia).

STERLING VINEYARDS

STERLING VINEYARDS
1111 Dunaweal Ln.
Calistoga, CA 94515
707-942-3345
800-726-6136
info@sterlingvineyards.com
www.sterlingvineyards.com

OWNER: Diageo Chateau
and Estate Wines.

LOCATION: 1 mile southeast
of Calistoga.

APPELLATION: Napa Valley.

HOURS: 10:30 A.M.– 5 P.M.,
Monday–Friday; 10 A.M.–
5 P.M. Saturday–Sunday.
10:30 A.M.–4:30 PM.
Monday–Sunday in winter.
Closed major holidays.

TASTINGS: $25 admission
for aerial tram ride,
self-guided tour, 5 wine
tastes, and souvenir glass.
For additional tastings of
reserve and limited-release
wines, visit the website.

TOURS: Self-guided.

THE WINES: Cabernet Franc,
Cabernet Sauvignon,
Chardonnay, Malvasia
Bianca, Merlot, Muscat
Canelli, Petite Sirah, Pinot
Gris, Pinot Noir, Sangiovese,
Sauvignon Blanc, Syrah,
Viognier, Zinfandel.

SPECIALTIES: Merlot, Cabernet
Sauvignon, Reserve SVR
(Bordeaux blend).

WINEMAKER: Mike Westrick.

ANNUAL PRODUCTION:
400,000 cases.

OF SPECIAL NOTE: Proceeds
from Wildlake Ranch
Merlot benefit the Napa
Land Trust. Summer movie
nights in the vineyard
on alternate Saturdays.
Display of Ansel Adams
photographs and wine-
related art.

NEARBY ATTRACTIONS:
Silverado Museum
(Robert Louis Stevenson
memorabilia); Napa Valley
Museum (winemaking
displays, art exhibits).

A commanding complex of bright white walls and curved bell towers, Sterling Vineyards rises from a forested volcanic knoll three hundred feet above the Napa Valley floor of the upper Napa Valley. The winery overlooks the valley from its location just south of Calistoga and offers sweeping vistas of the geometric vineyards and foothills below. To reach it, visitors leave their cars behind and board an aerial tramway—the only one of its kind in the valley—for a solar-powered glide over a glistening pond, pines, and live oaks to a walkway among the treetops.

A self-guided tour encourages visitors to explore the stately facility at their own pace, while strategically stationed hosts pour  wine samples along the way. Illustrated signboards describe points of interest, and motion-activated flat-screen televisions display winemaking activity. Bells from a tenth-century London church chime on the quarter hour, their rich tones ringing across exterior footpaths affording elevated views of the crush pad and fermentation area. Inside the winery, visitors may witness employees at work among stainless steel and redwood tanks, and peek at some of the winery's twenty-five thousand barrels as they impart delicate flavors to the wine aging within. On the Sterling View Terrace, redwood planters brim with lavender and ornamental grasses, and two sixty-foot-tall Italian cypresses frame the scene to the south. Here, guests sip wine as they take in the panoramic views of vineyards, neighboring estates, and Mount St. Helena, the Bay Area's tallest peak at just over 4,300 feet.

Englishman Peter Newton, founder of Sterling Paper International, started the winery in 1964, when he bought a fifty-acre pasture beside the town of Calistoga. He surprised local vintners by planting Merlot—at the time considered a minor blending grape—along with Chardonnay, Cabernet Sauvignon, and Sauvignon Blanc. In 1969 Newton bottled his first wines, which included California's earliest vintage-dated Merlot. In the early 1980s, the winery purchased one thousand acres of vineyard land on fourteen different Napa Valley ranches, giving the winemaker a broad spectrum of fruit to work with, as well as control over the farming of the grapes. The winery continues to source fruit from these and two hundred additional acres of select vineyards. The widely diverse appellations include Calistoga, St. Helena, Rutherford, Carneros, and the Oak Knoll and Diamond Mountain districts.

In 2001 a $14 million renovation of the visitor, tour, and tramway facilities was completed. Improvements included remilled oak flooring to replace 250 steps and the construction of three sleek new rooms to accommodate sit-down tastings of reserve and single-vineyard wines.

TWOMEY CELLARS

Twomey Cellars started out with a singular purpose: to produce handcrafted Merlot from just one vineyard, the Soda Canyon Ranch in southeastern Napa Valley. From the beginning, this intense focus has allowed winemaker Daniel Baron to practice painstaking, time-honored techniques that he believes maximize the inherent qualities of the grapes. Following the success of that first vintage in 1999, Twomey (pronounced "TOO-mee") has expanded its focus to include two other varietals, all the while remaining dedicated to making wines that reflect the best of their vineyard and vintage. In 2000 the winery acquired the West Pin Vineyard in the Russian River Valley of Sonoma County, an area acclaimed for extraordinary Pinot Noirs. The latest offering is Twomey Sauvignon Blanc, sourced from the winery's Napa Valley estate vineyard in Calistoga.

The original Twomey Cellars is located in the northern part of Napa Valley, where the gracious estate's courtyard has views of the Calistoga foothills. Opened in 2003, the stylish tasting room features slate floors and a sleek, curving bar, and is housed in one of two matching clapboard cottages that stand before the wine-making facility. The gleaming white buildings are surrounded by land-scaped gardens and flourishing Sauvignon Blanc vineyards. In 2007 Twomey Cellars opened a winery and tasting room on the west side of Healdsburg in Sonoma County, where its Sauvignon Blanc and Pinot Noirs are made.

Twomey Cellars, owned by the Duncan family of Silver Oak Cellars, continues to produce its flagship Merlot at the Calistoga winery. The 145-acre Soda Canyon Ranch, which remains the sole source for the wine, sits on deep, gravelly volcanic soil and is tightly planted with a particular strain of French Merlot clones. Selected for their low yield of small, intensely flavored berries, the mature vines have to struggle for nutrients. In addition, morning fog and the cool breezes wafting up from the northern reaches of San Francisco Bay create a temperate zone that extends the growing season without the risk of overripening the fruit. As a result, the Merlot ripens slowly enough to develop a pronounced rich black-fruit character. Soda Canyon Ranch produces a particularly complex Merlot that warrants meticulous handling by Baron, one of the few California winemakers versed in *soutirage traditional*, a slow, careful racking technique that decants the wine from one barrel to another without the disruptive effects of a pump. Baron learned this meticulous approach in Bordeaux, where *soutirage traditional* has been refined over centuries. The procedure, which allows the wine to flow by gravity or air pressure over eighteen months of aging, clarifies red wines to crystal-clear brilliance while drawing the fruit characteristics forward and softening the tannins.

TWOMEY CELLARS
1183 Dunaweal Ln.
Calistoga, CA 94515
707-942-2489
800-505-4850
info@twomeycellars.com
www.twomeycellars.com

OWNERS: Duncan family.

LOCATION: 2 miles south of Calistoga at Hwy. 29.

APPELLATION: Napa Valley.

HOURS: 9 A.M.–5 P.M. Monday–Saturday, 11 A.M.–5 P.M. Sunday, in summer; 9 A.M.–4 P.M. Monday–Saturday, 11 A.M.–4 P.M. Sunday, in winter.

TASTINGS: $10 (includes complimentary wineglass).

TOURS: Monday–Friday, reservations recommended. Saturday by appointment.

THE WINES: Merlot, Pinot Noir, Sauvignon Blanc.

SPECIALTY: Merlot.

WINEMAKER: Daniel Baron.

ANNUAL PRODUCTION: 15,000 cases.

OF SPECIAL NOTE: Latest vintage of Merlot is released each year on September 1 for limited distribution.

NEARBY ATTRACTIONS: Bothe-Napa State Park (hiking, picnicking, horseback riding, swimming Memorial Day–Labor Day); Robert Louis Stevenson State Park (hiking); Old Faithful Geyser of California; Petrified Forest; Sharpsteen Museum (exhibits on Walt Disney animator Ben Sharpsteen).

WHITEHALL LANE WINERY

WHITEHALL LANE WINERY
1563 Hwy. 29
St. Helena, CA 94574
800-963-9454
greatwine@whitehall
lane.com
www.whitehalllane.com

OWNER: Thomas Leonardini Sr.

LOCATION: 2 miles south of St. Helena.

APPELLATION: Rutherford.

HOURS: 10 A.M.–5:45 P.M. daily.

TASTINGS: $15 for current releases; price varies for reserve selections. No reservations required. Seated tastings by appointment.

TOURS: By appointment.

THE WINES: Cabernet Sauvignon, Chardonnay, dessert wine, Merlot, Pinot Noir, Sauvignon Blanc.

SPECIALTIES: Reserve Cabernet Sauvignon, Leonardini Vineyard Cabernet Sauvignon, Millennium MM Vineyard Cabernet Sauvignon.

WINEMAKER: Dean Sylvester.

ANNUAL PRODUCTION: 45,000 cases.

OF SPECIAL NOTE: Limited-production Leonardini Family Selection wines available only at the winery.

NEARBY ATTRACTIONS: Bothe-Napa State Park (hiking, picnicking, horseback riding, swimming Memorial Day–Labor Day; Culinary Institute of America at Greystone (cooking demonstrations); Silverado Museum (Robert Louis Stevenson memorabilia); Napa Valley Museum (winemaking displays, art exhibits).

Ocher and lavender, the colors of a California sunset, soften the geometric lines of Whitehall Lane, an angular, contemporary structure that stands in contrast to the pastoral setting of the vineyard. As if to telegraph the business at hand, the building's large windows have been cut in the shape of wine goblets. In front of the winery, a single row of square pillars runs alongside a walkway, each pillar supporting a vine that has entwined itself in the overhanging pergola.

Glass doors open into a tasting room that continues the overall theme with yellow walls, a white beamed ceiling, and a triptych painted with a stylized vineyard scene. The painting befits an estate where the first grapevines were planted in 1880. Even then, Napa Valley settlers were drawn to Rutherford's deep, loamy soils and sunny climate. A vestige of those days, a barn built for equipment storage, is still in use today.

In 1979 two brothers bought the twenty-six-acre vineyard and founded the winery they named after the road that runs along the south border of the property. They produced Merlot and Cabernet Sauvignon before selling the property nine years later. The Leonardini family of San Francisco took over the Whitehall Lane Estate in 1993. Tom Leonardini, already a wine aficionado, had been looking for property to purchase. He was aware of the winery's premium vineyard sources and some of its outstanding wines. Moreover, unlike his previous enterprises, the winery presented an opportunity to create a business that could involve his entire family.

Leonardini updated the winemaking and instituted a new barrel-aging program. He also re-planted the estate vineyard in Merlot and Sauvignon Blanc and began acquiring additional grape sources. Whitehall Lane now owns six Napa Valley vineyards, a total of 125 acres on the valley floor: the estate vineyard, the Millennium MM Vineyard, the Bommarito Vineyard, the Leonardini Vineyard, the Fawn Park Vineyard, and the Oak Glen Vineyard. The various wines produced from these vineyards were rated among the top five in the world on three occasions by *Wine Spectator* magazine.

Whitehall Lane's new building contains a barrel room and a crush pad, as well as a second-floor VIP tasting room. The goal of the facility is not to increase overall production, but to focus on small lots of Pinot Noir as well as wines produced from the St. Helena and Rutherford vineyards. As the winery approaches its thirty-second anniversary, the Leonardinis have many reasons to celebrate the success of their family business.

ZD WINES

ZD WINES
8383 Silverado Trail
Napa, CA 94558
800-487-7757
info@zdwines.com
www.zdwines.com

OWNERS: deLeuze family.

LOCATION: About 2.5 miles south of Zinfandel Ln.

APPELLATION: Rutherford.

HOURS: 10 A.M.–4:30 P.M. daily.

TASTINGS: $10 for 3 or 4 current releases; $15 for 2 or 3 reserve or older vintage wines.

TOURS: By appointment. Cellar Tour: $25; Eco Tour: $30; Vineyard View: $40.

THE WINES: Abacus (solera-style blend of ZD Reserve Cabernet Sauvignon), Cabernet Sauvignon, Chardonnay, Pinot Noir.

SPECIALTIES: Cabernet Sauvignon, Chardonnay, Pinot Noir.

WINEMAKERS: Robert deLeuze, wine master; Chris Pisani, winemaker; Brandon deLeuze, assistant winemaker.

ANNUAL PRODUCTION: 30,000 cases.

OF SPECIAL NOTE: Comprehensive tour and tasting of reserve wines with a focus on Abacus, $600 for 4 people minimum.

NEARBY ATTRACTIONS: Bothe-Napa State Park (hiking, picnicking, horseback riding, swimming Memorial Day–Labor Day); Silverado Museum (Robert Louis Stevenson memorabilia).

Driving along the Silverado Trail through the heart of Napa Valley, travelers are sure to notice the entrance to ZD Wines. A two-ton boulder, extracted from one of ZD's mountain vineyards, is adorned by the winery's striking gold logo, beckoning them to stop for a visit. Calla lilies intertwined with lavender welcome guests as they stroll to the winery entrance. The tasting room provides a cool respite on a hot summer day or a cozy place to linger in front of a fireplace in the winter. Behind the tasting bar are windows that allow visitors to peer into ZD's aging cellars as they sample ZD Chardonnay, Pinot Noir, and Cabernet Sauvignon.

It has been said that winemaking isn't rocket science, but in fact, founding partner Norman deLeuze had been designing liquid  rocket engines for Aerojet-General in Sacramento when he met his original partner Gino Zepponi. They decided to collaborate on producing classic Pinot Noir and Chardonnay varietals and needed a name for their new enterprise. The aeronautical industry had a quality-control program with the initials ZD, referring to Zero Defects. This matched the partners' initials and created a new association for the letters ZD. In 1969 the winery purchased Pinot Noir grapes from the Winery Lake Vineyard in Carneros in southern Sonoma and produced its first wine, the first ever labeled with the Carneros appellation. Soon after, the winery started making Chardonnay, which continues to be ZD's flagship wine.

Norman deLeuze turned to winemaking full-time, while his wife, Rosa Lee, handled sales and marketing. They purchased six acres, built their own winery, and planted Cabernet Sauvignon in Rutherford in 1979. Four years later, son Robert deLeuze was named winemaker. He had been working in ZD's cellars since he was twelve. In 2001 Robert passed the winemaking reins to Chris Pisani, who had worked closely with Robert for five years, building his appreciation and understanding of the family's consistent winemaking style.

Owned and operated by the deLeuzes for more than four decades, ZD Wines is a testament to the traditions, heritage, and passion of a true family business. Founders Norman and Rosa Lee's three children are currently at the helm of the winery: Julie deLeuze serves as administrative director; Robert deLeuze as CEO and wine master; and Brett deLeuze as president. Grandchildren Brandon and Jill deLeuze bring in the family's third generation as assistant winemaker and California sales/hospitality, respectively.

SONOMA

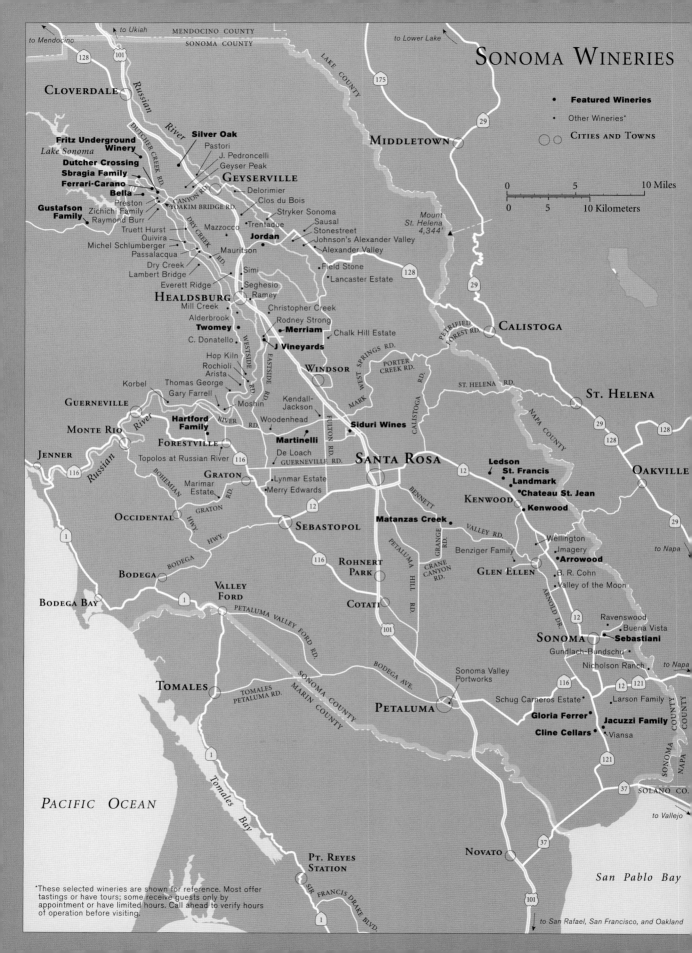

SONOMA WINERIES

● **Featured Wineries**
· Other Wineries*
○○ CITIES AND TOWNS

0 ——————— 5 ——————— 10 Miles
0 ———— 5 ———— 10 Kilometers

MENDOCINO COUNTY
SONOMA COUNTY

to Ukiah
to Mendocino
to Lower Lake

CLOVERDALE

MIDDLETOWN

Russian River
Lake Sonoma

Fritz Underground Winery
Dutcher Crossing
Sbragia Family
Ferrari-Carano
Bella
Gustafson Family
Preston
Zichichi Family
Raymond Burr
Truett Hurst
Quivira
Michel Schlumberger
Passalacqua
Dry Creek
Lambert Bridge
Everett Ridge

Silver Oak
Pastori
J. Pedroncelli
Geyser Peak
GEYSERVILLE
Delorimier
Clos du Bois
Stryker Sonoma
Sausal
Stonestreet
Johnson's Alexander Valley
Alexander Valley
Field Stone
Lancaster Estate

Mazzocco
Jordan
Mauritson
Simi
Seghesio
Ramey

Mount St. Helena 4,344'

CALISTOGA

ST. HELENA

HEALDSBURG
Mill Creek
Alderbrook
Twomey
C. Donatello
Hop Kiln
Rochioli
Arista
Thomas George
Gary Farrell
Moshin

Christopher Creek
Rodney Strong
Merriam
Chalk Hill Estate
J Vineyards

WINDSOR

Korbel
Kendall-Jackson
Woodenhead

GUERNEVILLE

MONTE RIO

Russian River

JENNER

Hartford Family
FORESTVILLE
Topolos at Russian River
GRATON
Marimar Estate
OCCIDENTAL

Lynmar Estate
Merry Edwards
De Loach
Martinelli

Siduri Wines

SANTA ROSA

Ledson
St. Francis
Landmark
Chateau St. Jean
KENWOOD
Kenwood

Matanzas Creek

Wellington
Imagery
Arrowood
B. R. Cohn
Valley of the Moon

SEBASTOPOL

BODEGA

ROHNERT PARK

Benziger Family
GLEN ELLEN

OAKVILLE

to Napa

BODEGA BAY

VALLEY FORD

COTATI

Ravenswood
Buena Vista
SONOMA
Sebastiani
Gundlach-Bundschu
Nicholson Ranch
to Napa

TOMALES

Sonoma Valley Portworks

PETALUMA

Schug Carneros Estate
Larson Family
Gloria Ferrer
Jacuzzi Family
Cline Cellars
Viansa

PACIFIC OCEAN

PT. REYES STATION

NOVATO

San Pablo Bay

SONOMA COUNTY
NAPA COUNTY

SOLANO CO.

to Vallejo

to San Rafael, San Francisco, and Oakland

*These selected wineries are shown for reference. Most offer tastings or have tours; some receive guests only by appointment or have limited hours. Call ahead to verify hours of operation before visiting.

S onoma boasts the greatest geographical diversity in California wine country. From the Pacific Coast to the inland valleys, to the Mayacamas Range that defines the eastern border with Napa County, the countryside is crisscrossed by dozens of rural roads, making it an ideal destination for casual exploration.

Most of the county's oldest wineries can be found in the historic town of Sonoma. Facing the extensively landscaped eight-acre central plaza are nineteenth-century adobe and false-front buildings that now house  upscale shops, restaurants, and inns, as well as historic sites.

In the northern part of the county, the city of Healdsburg has recently evolved from a quiet backwater into the hottest destination in Sonoma County. It sits at the hub of three major grape-growing regions—Russian River Valley, Alexander Valley, and Dry Creek Valley—all within a ten-minute drive of the vibrant town plaza.

North of Santa Rosa, the Russian River Valley extends from the Healdsburg area almost all the way to the ocean, where the Sonoma Coast has become one of the most sought-after wine appellations. In addition to the colorful villages clustered along the coastal routes, the region offers boating, swimming, and fishing opportunities and the shade of giant redwoods that soar above the Russian River's banks.

ARROWOOD VINEYARDS & WINERY

From the highway, the pair of gray, New England farmhouse–style buildings with generous porches neatly trimmed in white could easily pass for a country inn. In fact, the property was originally intended to become a bed-and-breakfast, but it never opened for business. Today, these handsome, sedate structures are home to the Arrowood Vineyards & Winery. The sweeping view from the wide porches encompasses the Arrowood vineyards, a neighboring winery, and the oak-studded slopes of Sonoma Mountain on the western horizon.

The winery's founder, Richard Arrowood, made his name as the longtime winemaker at Chateau St. Jean, just up the  road in Kenwood. A native San Franciscan raised in Santa Rosa, he earned degrees in both organic chemistry and enology, and got his start in the business in 1965 at Korbel Champagne Cellars. In 1974 the founders of Chateau St. Jean hired Arrowood as their first employee. For the next sixteen years, he made wines that earned both him and the winery worldwide attention.

In 1986 Richard and Alis Arrowood realized their lifelong dream of having their own winery, purchasing the property where Arrowood now sits. They designed their winery to blend harmoniously with the rural landscape. In 1990 Arrowood started to focus exclusively on reserve-quality Chardonnay and Cabernet Sauvignon. Before long, he was seduced by the idea of working with less common varietals, particularly when he found exceptional fruit. Today, Arrowood Vineyards produces Malbec, for instance, as well as more familiar wines, all made from Sonoma County grapes. The ten-acre estate vineyards, are farmed without the use of pesticides or herbicides, and in 2006 were certified organic by the California Certified Organic Farmers.

In 2010 Heidi von der Mehden, who joined Arrowood in 2007 as associate winemaker, was named head winemaker. Born in San Francisco, she grew up in Sonoma County. She left to study chemistry at Santa Clara University, after which she joined the Peace Corps and then taught chemistry to students in Tanzania. Returning to the United States, she immersed herself in the wine industry, working in a succession of wineries before coming to Arrowood and bringing a fresh enthusiasm to the winery's decades of accomplishments.

The spacious Hospitality House next to the winery has a dramatic vaulted ceiling, an enormous stone fireplace flanked by comfortable seating, and a second-floor loft for private events. Picture windows afford magnificent views of Sonoma Valley. Visitors are welcome to walk out the huge glass doors and relax on the wraparound veranda, wineglasses in hand.

ARROWOOD VINEYARDS & WINERY
14347 Hwy. 12
Glen Ellen, CA 95442
707-935-2600
hospitality@
arrowoodvineyards.com
www.arrowoodvineyards.
com

FOUNDERS: Richard and Alis Arrowood.

LOCATION: About 3 miles north of the town of Sonoma.

APPELLATION: Sonoma Valley.

HOURS: 10 A.M.–4:30 P.M. daily.

TASTINGS: $5 for 4 wines; $10 for 4 reserve wines.

TOURS: By appointment, 10:30 A.M. and 2:30 P.M. daily.

THE WINES: Cabernet Sauvignon, Chardonnay, Gewürztraminer, Malbec, Merlot, Pinot Blanc, red Rhône blend, Riesling (late harvest), Syrah, Viognier, white Rhône blend.

SPECIALTY: All wines are made from Sonoma County grapes.

WINEMAKER: Heidi von der Mehden.

ANNUAL PRODUCTION: 20,000 cases.

OF SPECIAL NOTE: Estate history tour and private tasting by appointment; events ranging from food-and-wine pairings to educational tastings. Wine accessories, gifts, and apparel sold at winery shop.

NEARBY ATTRACTION: Jack London State Historic Park (museum, hiking, horseback riding).

BELLA VINEYARDS AND WINE CAVES

**BELLA VINEYARDS
AND WINE CAVES**
9711 West Dry Creek Rd.
Healdsburg, CA 95448
707-473-9171
866-572-3552
info@bellawinery.com
www.bellawinery.com

OWNERS: Scott and Lynn
Adams.

LOCATION: 9 miles northwest
of Healdsburg via Dry
Creek Rd. and Yoakim
Bridge Rd.

APPELLATION: Dry Creek
Valley.

HOURS: 11 A.M.–4:30 P.M.
daily.

TASTINGS: $5.

TOURS: Cave and vineyard
tours by appointment.

THE WINES: Petite Sirah,
Syrah, Zinfandel, small lots
of Grenache.

SPECIALTIES: Vineyard-
designated Syrah, Zinfandel.

WINEMAKER: Joe Healy.

ANNUAL PRODUCTION:
7,500 cases.

OF SPECIAL NOTE:
Tasting room is in a 7,000-
square-foot cave. Picnic
area is partially shaded by
100-year-old olive trees.
Limits on the purchase of
specialty production wines.
Annual events include
Winter Wineland (January),
Barrel Tasting (March),
Passport to Dry Creek
Valley (April), Wine &
Food Affair (November).

NEARBY ATTRACTION:
Lake Sonoma (hiking,
fishing, boating, camping,
swimming).

Located on the banks of Dry Creek, this rustic winery has a fairy-tale quality. The refurbished, red-sided barn; the ancient olive trees with their giant, gnarled trunks; and the vineyards thriving above the cave entrance could be an illustration right out of an old-fashioned children's book.

The tale is a romantic one with a happily-ever-after ending. In 1994 Lynn and Scott Adams came to the Sonoma wine country to get married and fell in love all over again—with the land. They made another vow: to devote themselves to living in a rural setting and to making fine red wine. After all, Dry Creek Valley has long been famous for its abundance of very old Zinfandel vines known for producing small amounts of highly flavored grapes. A year later, the young couple bought their first Zinfandel vineyard on ninety-three acres at the western end of the valley. Before long, Lynn and Scott moved to the area to manage the property. They spent several years taking viticulture classes at the University of California, Davis, and elsewhere before they felt ready to make wine. By the time they opened the winery, they knew exactly what to call the place. Bella is named in honor of their first two daughters, who arrived around the same time as their first wine barrels.

To fully realize the rest of their dream—making small lots of fine Zinfandel and Syrah—the Adamses purchased two more low-yielding vineyards not far from their original property. The grapes for Bella's Grenache and estate Zinfandel come from eighty-five-year-old vines at Lily Hill Estate, as the original property is called. Bella also harvests Zinfandel from the Belle Canyon Vineyard on the east side of Dry Creek Valley, where old-clone, low-yielding vines deliver intensely flavored grapes. The third family vineyard, the Big River Ranch on the border of the Russian River and Alexander Valley appellations, is a veritable forest of hundred-year-old Zinfandel, Syrah, and Petite Sirah vines. Bella Vineyards does not need huge crops to make its wines—in fact, quite the opposite. The first vintage, 1999, consisted of only 200 cases. By focusing on single-vineyard wines and limiting production to a maximum of 7,500 cases, the Adamses have the option of postponing release dates until the wine is sufficiently aged and completely ready to drink.

As a family winery located on the quiet backroads of Dry Creek, Bella is appropriately low-key. Tastings are conducted inside the high-ceilinged aging caves, which are furnished with bistro tables and decorated with antique winery artifacts from around the world. The winery and its grounds are a popular destination for those looking for wonderful red wine and who, like Lynn and Scott Adams, find inspiration in the views of vineyards and rolling hills.

CHATEAU ST. JEAN WINERY

With the dramatic profile of Sugarloaf Ridge as a backdrop, the exquisitely landscaped grounds at Chateau St. Jean Winery in Kenwood evoke the image of a grand country estate. The château itself dates to the 1920s, but it wasn't until 1973 that a family of Central Valley, California, growers of table grapes founded the winery. They named it after a favorite relative and, with tongue in cheek, placed a statue of "St. Jean" in the garden.

The winery building was constructed from the ground up to suit Chateau St. Jean's particular style of winemaking. The founders believed in the European practice of creating vineyard-designated wines, so they designed the winery  to accommodate numerous lots of grapes, which could be kept separate throughout the wine- making process. Wines from each special vineyard are also bottled and marketed separately, with the vineyard name on the label. The winery produces a dozen vineyard- designated wines from the Sonoma Valley, Alexander Valley, Russian River Valley, and Carneros appella- tions. The winery also makes other premium varietals and one famously successful blend, the flagship Cinq Cépages Cabernet Sauvignon.

Chateau St. Jean became the first Sonoma winery to be awarded the prestigious Wine of the Year award from *Wine Spectator* magazine for its 1996 Cinq Cépages, a Bordeaux-style blend of five varieties, including Cabernet Sauvignon, Cabernet Franc, and Malbec. The winery received high acclaim again when it was given the #2 Wine of the Year award from *Wine Spectator* for its 1999 Cinq Cépages Cabernet Sauvignon. Winemaker Margo Van Staaveren has nearly thirty years of vineyard and winemaking experience with Chateau St. Jean, and her knowledge of Sonoma further underscores her excellence in highlighting the best of each vineyard.

In the summer of 2000, Chateau St. Jean opened the doors to its new Visitor Center and Gardens. A formal Mediterranean-style garden contains roses, herbs, and citrus trees planted in oversized terra-cotta urns arranged to create a number of open-air "rooms." Picnickers have always been welcome to relax on the winery's redwood-studded grounds, but now the setting is enhanced by the extensive plantings, making the one-acre garden attractive throughout the year.

Beyond the Mediterranean garden is the tasting room with a custom-made tasting bar. Fash- ioned from mahogany with ebony accents, the thirty-five-foot-long bar is topped with sheet zinc. The elegant château houses the Reserve Tasting Room. Visitors who would like to learn more about Chateau St. Jean wines are encouraged to make a reservation for a more in-depth program.

CHATEAU ST. JEAN WINERY
8555 Hwy. 12
Kenwood, CA 95452
707-833-4134
www.chateaustjean.com

OWNER: Treasury Wine Estates.

LOCATION: 8 miles east of Santa Rosa.

APPELLATION: Sonoma Valley.

HOURS: 10 A.M.–5 P.M. daily, except major holidays.

TASTINGS: $10 in main Tasting Room; $15 in Reserve Tasting Room.

TOURS: None.

THE WINES: Cabernet Franc, Cabernet Sauvi- gnon, Chardonnay, Fumé Blanc, Gewürztraminer, Malbec, Merlot, Pinot Blanc, Pinot Noir, Riesling, Syrah, Viognier.

SPECIALTIES: Cinq Cépages Cabernet Sauvignon and vineyard-designated wines.

WINEMAKER: Margo Van Staaveren.

ANNUAL PRODUCTION: 400,000 cases.

OF SPECIAL NOTE: Picnic tables in oak and redwood grove. Wine education classes. Open houses on most holidays. Store offering gourmet food and merchandise.

NEARBY ATTRACTION: Sugarloaf Ridge State Park (hiking, camping, horseback riding).

CLINE CELLARS

CLINE CELLARS
24737 Arnold Dr.
Sonoma, CA 95476
707-940-4030
www.clinecellars.com

OWNERS: Fred and Nancy Cline.

LOCATION: About 5 miles south of the town of Sonoma.

APPELLATION: Los Carneros.

HOURS: 10 A.M.–6 P.M. daily.

TASTINGS: Complimentary.

TOURS: 11 A.M., 1 P.M., and 3 P.M. daily.

THE WINES: Carignane, Marsanne, Mourvèdre, Pinot Gris, Syrah, Viognier, Zinfandel.

SPECIALTIES: Zinfandel, Rhône-style wines.

WINEMAKER: Charlie Tsegeletos.

ANNUAL PRODUCTION: Unavailable.

OF SPECIAL NOTE: Free museum displaying handcrafted models of California's Spanish missions, originally created for the 1939 World's Fair. Aviaries with exotic birds. Cookbooks, deli items, condiments, and gifts sold in winery shop.

NEARBY ATTRACTIONS: Mission San Francisco Solano and other historic buildings in downtown Sonoma; Infineon Raceway (NASCAR and other events); biplane flights; Cornerstone/Sonoma (garden installations and tours).

Five thousand rosebushes stand shoulder to shoulder beside the low stone wall that winds its way onto the winery grounds. From April through December, they provide a riot of fragrant pink, white, red, peach, lavender, and yellow blossoms. Picnic tables are scattered around the lawn, shaded by magnolias and other trees. Weeping willows hover over the mineral pools on either side of the restored 1850s farmhouse where the tasting room is located. The white farmhouse is rimmed with a picturesque dark green porch set with small wrought-iron tables and chairs where visitors can sip wine at their leisure.

Cline Cellars was originally established in Oakley, California, some forty miles east of San Francisco. Founder Fred Cline had spent his childhood summers learning about both farming and winemaking from his grandfather, Valeriano Jacuzzi (of spa and pump fame). Cline started the winery in 1982 with an inheritance from the sale of Jacuzzi Bros. In 1991 the Cline Cellars' facilities were relocated to this 350-acre estate in the Carneros appellation at the southern end of the Sonoma Valley.

The Cline estate occupies a historical parcel of land first settled by the Miwok Indians. Nearby, a nineteenth-century bathhouse harks to the time when the white settlers realized something that the Miwoks had known all along: warm mineral baths are good for you. While the town of Sonoma is generally considered the original site of the Sonoma mission, the mission was actually founded here when Father Altimira installed a cross on July 4, 1823. Perhaps it was the constant Carneros breezes that inspired him to pull up stakes and relocate to the town of Sonoma later that same year.

Cline Cellars specializes in Zinfandel and Rhône varietals. The winery's Zinfandel, Ancient Vines Carignane, and Mourvèdre wines are produced from some of the oldest and rarest vines in the state. The Sonoma location was selected especially for its relatively cool climate; chilly fog and frequent strong afternoon winds mitigate the summertime heat that blisters the rest of the Sonoma Valley. When the Clines bought the property, they planted all-new vineyards of Rhône varietals such as Syrah, Viognier, Marsanne, and Roussanne. Since 2000 the winery has practiced a high standard of sustainable and natural farming by following practices that give back to the land and create a self-nourishing ecosystem.

DUTCHER CROSSING WINERY

Dutcher Crossing Winery exemplifies the low-key ambience of Dry Creek Valley, an appellation sixteen miles long and at most two miles across that has been home to generations of grape growers and winemakers. Sited at a scenic junction of two creeks—Dry Creek and Dutcher Creek—the small winery has a quaint charm, and its architecture evokes the look of the farming community that first flourished here in the early 1900s. A wide breezeway between the tasting room and the winemaking building offers panoramic views of the valley's hillside beauty.

Purchased by Debra Mathy in 2007, Dutcher Crossing produces small-lot, vineyard-designated wines crafted by winemaker Kerry Damskey. In addition to the signature Cabernet Sauvignon–Syrah blend, he makes several Dry Creek

Valley Zinfandels, select Chardonnays from the Alexander Valley, and Pinot Noir sourced from the Russian River Valley. Over his thirty years as a winemaker, Damskey has become a leading proponent of blending; his Cabernet Sauvignon–Syrah is the first wine of its kind in Dry Creek Valley.

Proprietor Mathy expressed her adventuresome side by planting an estate vineyard block in the Châteauneuf-du-Pape style: a selection of Rhône varieties such as Grenache, Syrah, Mourvèdre, Cinsault, and Counoise. Guests can sip their selections while overlooking this planting from the trellised picnic area, set amid colorful gardens. Views of the valley landscape are also visible through the tall windows in the spacious tasting room, where highlights include a vaulted beam ceiling, a polished limestone tasting bar, and wide hickory plank floors. At one end of the rectangular room, a cozy conversation area with comfortable seating faces a fireplace made from locally quarried stone and topped with a mantel fashioned from distressed railroad ties. A vintage bicycle, the icon chosen to grace the redesigned Dutcher Crossing wine label, is also on display. It is a replica of an 1892 Rudge crafted in the classic Penny Farthing style so that the front is larger than the back.

Debra Mathy considers the bicycle a symbol of the timeless qualities of an artisan approach to life as well as to winemaking. As the last Christmas present she received from her late father, it also represents her journey to find Dutcher Crossing Winery. Mathy, an avid cyclist and lover of bicycles since childhood, spent ten years traveling with her father to discover the winery of their dreams. She can almost always be found during the day greeting visitors, with her golden lab, Dutchess, at her side. Their friendliness and enthusiasm reflect the culture and spirit of Dutcher Crossing.

DUTCHER CROSSING WINERY
8533 Dry Creek Rd.
Geyserville, CA 95441
707-431-2700
866-431-2711
info@dutchercrossing
winery.com
www.dutchercrossing
winery.com

OWNER: Debra Mathy.

LOCATION: 8.5 miles west of Dry Creek Valley exit off U.S. 101 via Dry Creek Rd.

APPELLATION: Dry Creek Valley.

HOURS: 11 A.M.–5 P.M. daily.

TASTINGS: $5 for 4-wine flight; $10 for reserve wine flight.

TOURS: ATV vineyard tours by appointment.

THE WINES: Cabernet Sauvignon, Chardonnay, Merlot, Petite Sirah, Port, Sauvignon Blanc, Syrah, Zinfandel.

SPECIALTY: Cabernet Sauvignon blend.

WINEMAKER: Kerry Damskey.

ANNUAL PRODUCTION: 7,000 cases.

OF SPECIAL NOTE: Picnic tables (reservations for parties of six or more) and *pétanque* court; limited deli selections available. Select wines sold only at tasting room.

NEARBY ATTRACTION: Lake Sonoma (swimming, fishing, boating, hiking, camping).

FERRARI-CARANO VINEYARDS & WINERY

FERRARI-CARANO VINEYARDS & WINERY
8761 Dry Creek Rd.
Healdsburg, CA 95448
707-433-6700
customerservice@
ferrari-carano.com
www.ferrari-carano.com

OWNERS: Don and Rhonda Carano.

LOCATION: 9 miles west of U.S. 101 via Dry Creek Rd. exit.

APPELLATION: Dry Creek Valley.

HOURS: 10 A.M.–5 P.M. daily.

TASTINGS: $5 for 4 classic wines; $15 for 4 reserve wines (applicable to wine purchase). $20–$35 for private tastings, Monday–Saturday, by appointment.

TOURS: Monday–Saturday, 10 A.M., by appointment (800-831-0381).

THE WINES: Cabernet Sauvignon, Chardonnay, Late Harvest Black Muscat, Late Harvest Semillon, Merlot, Muscat Canelli, Pinot Grigio, Pinot Noir, Sangiovese, Sauvignon Blanc, Syrah, Zinfandel.

SPECIALTIES: PreVail (Cabernet Sauvignon), Siena (Sangiovese blend), Trésor (Bordeaux-style blend).

WINEMAKERS: Sarah Quider, Aaron Piotter.

ANNUAL PRODUCTION: About 200,000 cases.

OF SPECIAL NOTE: Enoteca reserve tasting bar open daily. Tulip hotline: 707-433-5349.

NEARBY ATTRACTION: Lake Sonoma (fishing, boating, hiking).

Don and Rhonda Carano were introduced to Sonoma County in 1979 while searching for wines to enhance the award-winning wine lists of their hotel, the Eldorado, in Reno, Nevada. The Caranos, both second-generation Italian Americans, were struck by the natural beauty of the area and decided to purchase a seventy-acre parcel in Alexander Valley that came with a 1904 farmhouse and thirty acres of grapevines.

The acquisition piqued their curiosity about winemaking, and they began taking courses on enology and viticulture at the University of California, Davis. Realizing the potential for the area, the Caranos began to acquire vineyard land in five appellations: Alexander Valley, Russian River Valley, Dry Creek Valley, Anderson Valley, and Carneros. In 1981 the couple founded Ferrari-Carano Vineyards & Winery at the western end of Dry Creek Road in Dry Creek Valley. Six years later, the first wines bearing the Ferrari-Carano label, the 1986 Fumé Blanc and the 1985 Alexander Valley Chardonnay, were released. Today, Ferrari-Carano produces those wines, as well as a variety of other whites and reds, including such specialties as Siena (a Sangiovese-based blend), Trésor (a Bordeaux-style blend), and vineyard-select Chardonnays from Russian River Valley.

In 1997 the Caranos completed Villa Fiore (House of Flowers), the winery's magnificent hospitality center. The 25,000-square-foot Italianate-style building has dramatic stone arches and columns, sienna-colored stucco walls, a tile roof, and limestone accents throughout. Upon entering the center, visitors find an Italian-Mediterranean décor that includes a coffered ceiling of hand-tooled bird's-eye maple, marbleized walls and flooring, and a tasting bar that overlooks the vineyards. A curving stone staircase leads to the barrel cellar where classic columns support a double-vaulted ceiling. A subterranean space, called Enoteca (Italian for "wine library"), has a number of opulent features: a thirty-seven-foot barrel-shaped tasting bar with a black granite top and a dramatic, glass-enclosed wine bottle cellar running the length of the bar. Visitors may taste Ferrari-Carano's limited-production and reserve wines in this elegant space.

The winery is surrounded by five acres of spectacular gardens designed by Rhonda Carano. What began in 1997 as a labor of love took sixteen months just to plan and complete the initial planting. Visitors are invited to stroll the meandering paths and footbridges along a rippling stream captured at both ends by waterfalls that flow into fish ponds. The stunning gardens change color schemes with every season. In the spring, more than 10,000 tulips and daffodils take center stage. Visitors may call the winery for information on the timing of this beautiful display.

FRITZ UNDERGROUND WINERY

What began as an idyllic family retreat is now a thriving family business on the northern edge of Dry Creek Valley. Jay and Barbara Fritz were seeking an escape from the summertime fog and urban bustle of San Francisco when they found this rugged, hundred-plus-acre property on a remote hillside back in 1970. They dammed a spring to create "Lake Fritz" and built a home away from home. Son Clayton Fritz and his siblings spent childhood summers in this picturesque setting. But it has been a long time since Clayton Fritz swam in the pond. Now, as president of the winery, he is far too busy looking after the day-to-day operations.

Construction of the winery began in 1979, when energy crises were commonplace. The idea of creating an energy-efficient, subterranean winery seemed logical, especially given the capacity to construct a gravity-flow production system. The unique three-tier structure allows crushing to be done on top of the winery, and from there the juice is sent underground to the level containing the fermentation tanks. When the time is ripe, small lots of wine are sent a level deeper. White wines are aged in an underground barrel room, and red wines mature in the adjoining cave that stretches two hundred feet into the mountain. This gravity system eliminates the need for pumping equipment and therefore less agitation of the wine. Because the facility is underground and maintains a constant temperature of fifty-eight degrees Fahrenheit, there is no need for air-conditioning. Refrigeration is required only to cool the fermentation tanks.

The winery's focus is on small-production estate vineyard and single-vineyard-designated wines, many of which are available only at the winery. Fruit for the Sauvignon Blanc, Zinfandel, Cabernet Sauvignon, Malbec, and Petit Verdot comes from the Dry Creek estate vineyards. Source for the Chardonnay, Pinot Noir, and Syrah is the Russian River Valley, where the cooler climate regulates the ripening of these Burgundian varietals.

Upon ascending the hill to the winery, visitors discover an inviting tasting room with a picturesque patio, where they can enjoy a picnic under the shade of market umbrellas and a beautiful view of Lake Fritz. Rockroses and other hardy plants grow in handsome terraces and give way to wild grasses as the hill slopes down to the water's edge. Visitors can make a weekend appointment for a tour of the underground facilities, where they may be treated to a special barrel tasting of one of the aging wines.

FRITZ UNDERGROUND WINERY
24691 Dutcher Creek Rd.
Cloverdale, CA 95425
707-894-3389
800-418-9463
info@fritzwinery.com
www.fritzwinery.com

PRESIDENT:
Clayton B. Fritz.

LOCATION: About 1 mile
southwest of intersection
of U.S. 101 and Dutcher
Creek Rd.

APPELLATION: Dry Creek
Valley.

HOURS: 10:30 A.M.–
4:30 P.M. daily.

TASTINGS: $10 (applicable
to wine purchase).

TOURS: By appointment.

THE WINES: Cabernet
Sauvignon, Chardonnay,
Estate Zinfandel, Late-
Harvest Zinfandel, Pinot
Noir, Rosé, Sauvignon
Blanc, Syrah.

SPECIALTIES: Cabernet
Sauvignon, Chardonnay,
Pinot Noir, Zinfandel.

ANNUAL PRODUCTION:
18,000 cases.

OF SPECIAL NOTE:
Patio for picnicking.
Annual events include
Winter Wineland
(January), Barrel Tasting
(March), Dry Creek
Passport Weekend (April).
Late-Harvest Zinfandel,
Ruxton Chardonnay, and
Syrah available only at
winery.

NEARBY ATTRACTIONS:
Russian River (swimming,
canoeing, kayaking,
rafting, fishing); Lake
Sonoma (boating,
camping, hiking, fishing).

GLORIA FERRER CAVES & VINEYARDS

**GLORIA FERRER
CAVES & VINEYARDS**
23555 Hwy. 121
Sonoma, CA 95476
707-996-7256
info@gloriaferrer.com
www.gloriaferrer.com

OWNERS: Ferrer family.

LOCATION: 4 miles south of
the town of Sonoma.

APPELLATION: Los Carneros.

HOURS: 10 A.M.–5 P.M. daily.

TASTINGS: $5–10 per glass
of sparkling wine; $2–3 for
estate varietal wine.

TOURS: Daily during hours
of operation.

THE WINES: Blanc de Noirs,
Brut, Chardonnay, Merlot,
Pinot Noir.

SPECIALTIES: Brut Rosé,
Carneros Cuvée, Gravel
Knob Vineyard Pinot Noir,
José S. Ferrer Reserve,
Royal Cuvée, Rust Rock
Terrace Pinot Noir,
Va de Vi sparkling wine.

WINEMAKER: Bob Iantosca.

ANNUAL PRODUCTION:
150,000 cases.

OF SPECIAL NOTE: Spanish
cookbooks and locally
made products, as well
as deli items, sold at the
winery. Annual Catalan
Festival (July).

NEARBY ATTRACTIONS:
Mission San Francisco
Solano and other historic
buildings in downtown
Sonoma; Infineon
Raceway (NASCAR and
other events); biplane
flights; Cornerstone/
Sonoma (garden
installations and tours).

The Carneros appellation, with its continual winds and cool marine air, is known far and wide as an ideal climate for growing Pinot Noir and Chardonnay grapes. The word spread all the way to Spain, where the Ferrer family had been making sparkling wine for more than a century. The Ferrers are the world's largest producer of sparkling wine.

Members of the family had been looking for vineyard land in the United States off and on for fifty years when José and Gloria Ferrer visited the southern part of the Sonoma Valley. The climate reminded them of their Catalan home in Spain, and in 1982, they acquired a forty-acre pasture and then, four years later, another two hundred acres nearby. They started planting vineyards with Pinot Noir and Chardonnay, the traditional sparkling wine grapes. The winery now cultivates nearly four hundred acres in Carneros and, in addition to spar-kling wines, produces still wines, including Pinot Noir, Merlot, and Chardonnay. Gloria Ferrer wines have a history of critical success. Within a year of its 1986 debut, the winery won seven gold medals, marking the beginning of many acco-lades to come. Since 2005, the wines have received more than 250 gold medals.

The winery that José Ferrer built was the first sparkling wine house in Carneros. Named for his wife, it was designed after a *masia* (a Catalan farmhouse), complete with terraces, a red tile roof, and thick walls the color of the Spanish plains. Complementing the exterior, the winery's cool interior has tile floors and Spanish antiques. The ties to Spain continue in the winery's shop, which offers a selection of cookbooks devoted to Spanish cuisine and the specialties of Catalonia. Also available are several Sonoma-grown products such as Gloria Ferrer's sparkling wine–filled chocolates, and both local and Spanish cheeses, as well as other Spanish delicacies.

Visitors are welcome to enjoy Gloria Ferrer wines, both still and sparkling, in the spacious tasting room or outside on the Vista Terrace. There they are treated to a breathtaking view of Carneros and the upper reaches of San Pablo Bay. On a clear day, they can see all the way to the peak of 3,848-foot Mount Diablo in the East Bay. Both still and sparkling wines are aged in the caves tunneled into the hill behind the hospitality center.

Tours of the winery include a visit to these aromatic dark recesses, where guides explain the traditional *méthode champenoise* process of creating sparkling wine, during which the wine undergoes its secondary fermentation in the bottle—the one that forms the characteristic bubbles.

D. H. Gustafson Family Vineyard

On a quiet country road winding through the foothills above Dry Creek Valley, D. H. Gustafson Family Vineyard sits at a lofty 1,800 feet above sea level. Seemingly remote, yet less than thirty minutes from Healdsburg, this crowd-free getaway offers intimate wine tastings and a tranquil spot for a picnic. Ancient madrones and oaks blanket the 247-acre property with a year-round canopy of green. From the winery, panoramic views include Napa County thirty miles to the east, and Mount St. Helena. At the rustic hilltop picnic area, visitors can see the Mayacamas Range in the distance and shimmering Lake Sonoma.

With twenty acres of vineyards ranging in elevation from 1,600 to 1,800 feet, the former sheep ranch is one of the highest elevation  wineries in Sonoma County. Owner Dan Gustafson, a Minnesota farm boy who became a prominent real estate developer and landscape architect, purchased the property in 2002 and planted his vineyards with an eye to preserving the natural features, while leaving the rest of the property as an ecological preserve. Local lore relates that where madrones grow, so will grapes, and the region's red volcanic soil provides the quick drain- age grapes prefer and the lean, dry conditions that produce small berries with concentrated flavors.

Farming practices are strictly sustainable and include the use of blando brome, an annual grass, and red clover as cover crops to replenish the soil. The vineyards grow within a ten-minute walk of the winery, allowing winemaker Emmett Reed to inspect the rows daily. Consulting winemaker Kerry Damskey, noted for making stylish red wines from high-elevation vineyards, works closely with Reed, who lives on the property and oversees the vineyard and the winemaking process. Together, they create memorable wines—made entirely from handpicked estate fruit—ranging from crisp Riesling to bold Zinfandel.

The stunning house was designed by architect Tim Bjella to wed visually with the site. The red stone foundation matches the color of the soil, and the curves and angles of the roofline mirror the rolling hills in the valley below. The square tower rising dramatically from the center of the residence appears in a stylized version on the winery's label. The intimate tasting room is often staffed by owner Dan Gustafson, winemaker Emmett Reed, or tasting room manager Kaitlin Reed. The space has a concrete bar, tall black leather chairs, and display shelves built from reclaimed wood. In this inviting room, midwestern hospitality prevails amid the mountain air and rural hush of Sonoma County's high country.

D. H. Gustafson Family Vineyard
9100 Skaggs Springs Rd.
Geyserville, CA 95441
707-433-2371
info@gfvineyard.com
www.gfvineyard.com

Owners: Dan, Kristen, and Jeff Gustafson.

Location: 17 miles northwest of Healdsburg.

Appellation: Dry Creek Valley.

Hours: 10 A.M.–4 P.M. Saturday, or by appointment.

Tastings: Complimentary.

Tours: Guided tours of winery and vineyard ($25), including tasting, by reservation.

The Wines: Estate-grown Cabernet Sauvignon, Petite Sirah, Riesling, Rosé of Syrah, Sauvignon Blanc, Syrah, Zinfandel.

Specialties: Petite Sirah, Late Harvest Red (Port-style dessert wine), Zinfandel.

Winemaker: Emmett Reed; consulting winemaker: Kerry Damskey.

Annual Production: 4,000 cases.

Of Special Note: A 300-year-old, 11-foot-diameter madrone on property is believed to be the largest madrone in Sonoma County. Picnic area with panoramic views of Lake Sonoma. Oil made from estate olives available in tasting room. Dry Creek Winegrowers Association Passport event held the last weekend in April.

Nearby Attraction: Lake Sonoma (swimming, fishing, boating, camping, hiking).

HARTFORD FAMILY WINERY

HARTFORD FAMILY WINERY
8075 Martinelli Rd.
Forestville, CA 95436
707-887-8011
800-588-0234, ext. 8030
hartford.winery@
hartfordwines.com
www.hartfordwines.com

OWNERS: Don and Jennifer
Hartford.

LOCATION: 2 miles
northwest of Forestville.

APPELLATION: Russian River
Valley.

HOURS: 10 A.M.–4:30 P.M.
daily.

TASTINGS: $5 for 3
wines; $15 for 6 wines.
Reservations required
for groups of 6 or more.
$25 for Seated Private
Library Tasting of 6 wines;
$45 for Private Wine
Seminar and Artisan
Cheese Experience.
Reservations required.

TOURS: $10, by
appointment.

THE WINES: Chardonnay,
Pinot Noir, Zinfandel.

SPECIALTIES: Single-
vineyard Chardonnay,
Pinot Noir, and old-vine
Zinfandel.

WINEMAKER: Jeff Mangahas.

ANNUAL PRODUCTION:
12,000–15,000 cases.

OF SPECIAL NOTE: Shaded
picnic area with tables.
Zinfandel Port and most
single-vineyard wines only
available in tasting room.

NEARBY ATTRACTIONS:
Russian River (rafting,
fishing, swimming,
canoeing, kayaking);
Armstrong Redwoods
State Reserve (hiking,
horseback riding); Laguna
de Santa Rosa (freshwater
wetlands with wildlife
viewing).

Toyon, oak, and coast redwood fringe the sinuous country road that leads to the home of Hartford Family Winery. At the driveway, a one-lane bridge crosses Green Valley Creek into a forest clearing where the château-style winery offers a peaceful retreat. Sycamores shade the stately complex, and a fountain bubbles opposite the double doors of the tasting room. Furnished with European antiques, the spacious foyer opens into a space with crisp white cabinetry and a French limestone floor.

Renowned for crafting single-vineyard Chardonnay, Pinot Noir, and old-vine Zinfandel, the winery was founded in 1993 by Don and Jennifer Hartford. Don, whose family farmed strawberries in western Mas-sachusetts, had recently con-cluded a successful law practice in Northern California and was drawn to the viticulture of Russian River Valley. With help from Jennifer's father, Jess Jackson, cofounder of Kendall-Jackson Wine Estates, the couple purchased the winery property about a dozen miles northwest of Santa Rosa.

Of the winery's ten Pinot Noir offerings, nine are strikingly diverse single-vineyard bottlings made from 95 percent estate fruit. The estate vineyards thrive in five appellations: Los Carneros, Anderson Valley, Sonoma Coast, Russian River Valley, and Green Valley. All are cool-climate sites that yield small crops of often late-ripening grapes treasured for their flawless varietal flavors. The blended Land's Edge Pinot Noir is sourced from estate vineyards located in Annapolis, on the Sonoma coast, some thirty miles north of the tasting room. For Chardonnay, the winery turns to the Sonoma Coast and Russian River Valley appellations. About half the fruit is harvested from estate vineyards, including Laura's Vineyard, planted with rare, old-clone Chardonnay, and Seascape Vineyard, a six-acre ridgetop site facing Bodega Bay. The Hartfords craft five single-vineyard and one blended Zinfandel, all from dry-farmed Russian River Valley vines boasting an average age of eighty-five years. The grapes from these august vines exhibit rich berry and spice components borne of both the vines' great age and the region's relatively chilly, protracted growing season.

The single-vineyard wines are made in limited lots, some as small as a hundred cases. During harvest, all the fruit is handpicked and then sorted by hand to remove everything but the best berries. Using only French oak barrels, the winemaker selects from twelve different cooperages, matching barrels to each lot of wine to elevate the expression of both vineyard site and varietal characteristics.

J VINEYARDS & WINERY

Judy Jordan founded J Vineyards & Winery in 1986, three years after Russian River Valley was proclaimed a distinct winegrowing appellation. She was already familiar with the land, the climate, and the grapes—notably Chardonnay and Pinot Noir—for which the appellation is internationally acclaimed. Those are the two primary grapes that go into sparkling wine, which quickly became the winery's major focus.

What began as a small *méthode champenoise* sparkling wine project at her father Tom Jordan's winery on the other side  of Healdsburg has become a model for Russian River Valley sparkling and varietal winemaking. To that end, Judy Jordan hired her longtime friend George Bursick as winemaker in 2006. Bursick, who had spent the past twenty-one years making wines at Ferrari-Carano, immediately took steps to realize Jordan's goal of expanding the winery's portfolio with more *terroir*-driven, small-production bottlings of Pinot Noir, a grape that is famously delicate and prone to sunburn except when grown in areas such as Russian River Valley, which enjoys the moderating effects of the river itself.

J Vineyards & Winery has long been recognized as a pioneer among American wineries in promoting wine paired with food. Sampling Pinot Noir with licorice-braised Painted Hills beef short rib or Pinot Gris with duck rillettes, quince compote, and Forelle pears creates an indelible memory of how the right combinations bring out the best in both food and wine. Executive chef Mark Caldwell creates a variety of seasonal delights to pair with J's food-friendly varietal and sparkling wines in three different formats that augment the wine-only tastings available in the J Signature Bar.

Judy Jordan continues to evolve the hospitality experience at J Vineyards & Winery. The wine-and-food pairings are now held in three distinct venues designed to enhance the experience, while the tasting room is devoted exclusively to J's Russian River Valley wines.

In the ultra-contemporary tasting room, guests are served at the J Signature Bar that extends across the back of the spacious room. Behind it is an enormous, eye-catching wall in which bubbles appear to be rising. This work of art in jagged glass and fiber optics, as well as the rest of the art in the tasting room, was designed by noted regional artist Gordon Huether. In addition, exquisitely designed wine accessories and stemware from luxury designers, as well as imported serving pieces, fine linens, papers, and gourmet condiments, complement J's commitment to creating the best environment to experience wine with food.

J VINEYARDS & WINERY
11447 Old Redwood Hwy.
Healdsburg, CA 95448
707-431-3646
888-594-6326
info@jwine.com
www.jwine.com

OWNER: Judy Jordan.

LOCATION: About 3 miles south of Healdsburg.

APPELLATION: Russian River Valley.

HOURS: 11 A.M.–5 P.M. daily.

TASTINGS: $20 for 5 wines. Reserve tastings with food pairings: Outdoor Terrace, $35, Friday–Monday, 11 A.M.–4 P.M.; Bubble Room, $60, Thursday–Tuesday, 11 A.M.–4 P.M.; Essence, $200 (7 wines paired with a 7-course luncheon plus tour), Thursday, 11 A.M.–3 P.M.

TOURS: By appointment, 11 A.M. and 2:30 P.M. daily.

THE WINES: Brut and Rosé sparkling wines, Chardonnay, Pinotage, Pinot Noir, Ratafia (dessert wine), Vin Gris, Viognier, Zinfandel.

SPECIALTIES: Cool-climate, site-specific Russian River Valley Pinot Noir and Chardonnay; *méthode champenoise* sparkling wines.

WINEMAKER: George Bursick.

ANNUAL PRODUCTION: 60,000 cases.

OF SPECIAL NOTE: Annual events include Varietal Release (May).

NEARBY ATTRACTION: Russian River (swimming, canoeing, kayaking, rafting, fishing).

JACUZZI FAMILY VINEYARDS

JACUZZI FAMILY VINEYARDS
24724 Arnold Dr.
Sonoma, CA 95476
707-931-7575
www.jacuzziwines.com

OWNERS: Fred and Nancy Cline.

LOCATION: About 5 miles south of the town of Sonoma.

APPELLATION: Los Carneros.

HOURS: 10 A.M.–5:30 P.M. daily.

TASTINGS: Complimentary.

TOURS: Available upon request ($15–$25).

THE WINES: Aglianico, Aleatico, Arneis, Barbera, Cabernet Sauvignon, Chardonnay, Dolcetto, Lagrein, Merlot, Muscato Bianco, Nebbiolo, Nero d'Avola, Pinot Grigio, Pinot Noir, Primitivo, Sagrantino, Sangiovese, Valeriano, Vernaccia.

SPECIALTIES: Italian varietals.

WINEMAKER: Charlie Tsegeletos.

ANNUAL PRODUCTION: Unavailable.

OF SPECIAL NOTE: Most wines sold only at winery. Courtyard tables with market umbrellas for picnics. Cookbooks, specialty foods, home décor items, and gifts sold in winery shop. The Olive Press, producer of oil from local olives, is on-site.

NEARBY ATTRACTIONS: Mission San Francisco Solano in downtown Sonoma; Schellville Airport (biplane rides); Cornerstone/Sonoma (garden installations and tours).

The winery's rustic stone-and-plaster exterior offers visitors their first hint of the Jacuzzi family's long, rich history, which reaches back to the Friuli region of northeastern Italy. The unmatched facades on either side of the entry are intentional: the building was designed after the family's ancestral home, created over time by various artisans using slightly different stones. Although the 18,000-square-foot winery was completed in 2007, the use of traditional architectural detailing, natural materials, and a variety of roof forms purposefully creates the impression that it was built centuries ago.

The complex of similar, small structures is organized around a central courtyard that provides the inviting ambience associated with the sharing of food, wine, and hospitality. The winery, like many of the wines themselves, pays homage to the Jacuzzi family's parents, two siblings among seven brothers and six sisters who arrived in the United States in the early twentieth century and went on to achieve great success in their new country.

Inside the stately entrance, monastery-like white walls soar to rustic beamed ceilings in the spacious hall. To the left is the tasting room, which has a bar made of downed oak and walnut trees from Sonoma Valley. The slats of wood below the surface of the tasting bar have been fashioned to look like the curved staves of wine barrels. True to the family's commitment to hospitality, tastings of the winery's many Italian varietal wines are complimentary.

Wide hallways lead to an interior courtyard typical of vernacular Friuli architecture. Here, several tables graced with market umbrellas offer expansive views of the vineyards. The courtyard faces a spectacular marble fountain, where a larger-than-life figure of Neptune arises triumphantly among gigantic, water-spouting horses.

Nearby, stairs climb to a viewing area overlooking the San Pablo Bay wetlands and distant mountains. The second floor is also home to an informal family museum where photographs and other memorabilia commemorate the Jacuzzi legacy of innovation. An early invention was the so-called toothpick propeller, made of laminated wood and utilized on World War I airplanes. Fred Cline, cofounder of both Jacuzzi Family Vineyards and Cline Cellars across the road, is the maternal grandson of Valeriano Jacuzzi, one of the seven brothers who participated in the creation of the spa that bears the family name. What turned out to be a revolutionary concept started in 1948 when the brothers figured out how to treat a family member's rheumatoid arthritis with a hydrotherapy pump, leading to the family's most famous invention and the launching of a major industry.

JORDAN VINEYARD & WINERY

Parts of Sonoma County resemble the French wine country, but mostly in a topographical sense. The picture always lacked a key element: a grand château. That changed in 1972, when Tom Jordan established his estate in Alexander Valley. Inspired by several eighteenth-century châteaus in southwestern France, the winery, situated on an oak-studded knoll, was designed by the San Francisco architectural firm of Backen, Arrigoni & Ross. The château, with its classic wine-red doors and shutters, also serves as a visual metaphor for the winemaking philosophy at Jordan, where Cabernet Sauvignon and Chardonnay are crafted in the French tradition with the hallmarks of balance, elegance, and food affinity.

As visitors approach on the winding driveway, they are teased with glimpses of the château until they reach the top of the hill and can see the entire structure and its landscaped grounds. The image of an old-world estate is furthered by the formal French gardens with their clipped pollarded sycamores. Boston privet hedges, poplar trees, and changes colors with the seasons. ivy clinging to the château walls bronze statue of Bacchus, a Gracing the entrance is a small Tatti's 1512 original in the copy of Jacopo Sansovino From the hilltop, every vantage National Museum in Florence. Alexander Valley and its most affords panoramic vistas of dramatic focal points, Geyser

Peak and Mount St. Helena. It was ancient volcanic activity from Geyser Peak, along with eons of seismic uplift, that formed the narrow, twenty-mile-long valley named for the pioneering family who began farming this area in 1847.

By 1974 Tom Jordan had acquired more than 1,500 acres, which included two lakes and plenty of room for the château and winery facility. After an enlightening trip to Italy in 1995, he planted the first grove of Tuscan olive trees, whose fruit is pressed for the winery's award-winning estate extra-virgin olive oil. Then, in 2005, after taking the helm of the family winery, son John embarked on various initiatives to enhance the winemaking and sustainable farming practices while reducing the winery's carbon footprint.

The winery also elevated its hospitality experience for visitors. Each tour culminates with a tasting of current releases, a library wine, and a selection of artisan cheeses in the comfortable cellar room. Guests are welcome to enjoy intimate seated tastings without the tour.

JORDAN VINEYARD & WINERY
1474 Alexander Valley Rd.
Healdsburg, CA 95448
707-431-5250
800-654-1213
info@jordanwinery.com
www.jordanwinery.com

OWNER: John Jordan.

LOCATION: About 4 miles northeast of Healdsburg.

APPELLATION:
Alexander Valley.

HOURS: 8 A.M.–4:30 P.M. Monday–Friday; 9 A.M.– 3:30 P.M. Saturday. Open Sundays May–October.

TASTINGS: By appointment.

TOURS: By appointment.

THE WINES: Cabernet Sauvignon, Chardonnay.

SPECIALTIES: Alexander Valley Cabernet Sauvignon, Russian River Chardonnay.

WINEMAKER: Rob Davis.

ANNUAL PRODUCTION: 90,000 cases.

OF SPECIAL NOTE: Extensive landscaped grounds and gardens, including Tuscan olive trees. Jordan estate extra-virgin olive oil sold at winery. Library, dessert, and large-format wines available only at winery.

NEARBY ATTRACTIONS: Lake Sonoma (boating, camping, hiking, fishing, swimming); Jimtown Store (country market, homemade foods).

KENWOOD VINEYARDS

KENWOOD VINEYARDS
9592 Hwy. 12
Kenwood, CA 95452
707-833-5891
info@heckestates.com
www.kenwoodvineyards.com

OWNER: F. Korbel & Bros.

LOCATION: 10 miles southeast of Santa Rosa.

APPELLATION: Sonoma Valley.

HOURS: 10 A.M.–4:30 P.M. daily.

TASTINGS: $5 (refundable with purchase of 3 bottles of wine).

TOURS: None.

THE WINES: Cabernet Sauvignon, Chardonnay, Gewürztraminer, Merlot, Pinot Noir, Sauvignon Blanc, sparkling wines, White Zinfandel, Zinfandel.

SPECIALTIES: Artist Series, Jack London Ranch wines.

WINEMAKER: Pat Henderson.

ANNUAL PRODUCTION: 550,000 cases.

OF SPECIAL NOTE: Occasional themed food-and-wine events matching chef's specialties with appropriate wines. Limited-release Artist Series wines available only at winery.

NEARBY ATTRACTIONS: Jack London State Historic Park (museum, hiking, horseback riding); Sugarloaf Ridge State Park (hiking, camping, horseback riding).

The photogenic, century-old barn where visitors come to taste Kenwood's wines dates to one of the most romantic eras in Sonoma Valley history. The quintessential adventure author Jack London was living, writing, and raising grapes in nearby Glen Ellen when the Pagani Brothers established their winery in 1906 in the buildings that now house Kenwood Vineyards. In those days, long before the invention of tasting rooms, wine lovers would bring their own barrels and jugs to be filled and then cart them home.

Decades later, in 1970, a trio of wine enthusiasts from the San Francisco Bay Area founded Kenwood Vineyards. In redesigning and modernizing the existing winery, they created a facility that allows the winemaker the utmost in flexibility. More than 125 stainless steel ferment-ing and upright oak tanks are utilized in combination with some seventeen thousand French and American oak barrels. Kenwood uses estate fruit as well as grapes from some of Sonoma County's best vineyards and follows the cuvée winemaking method, in which the harvest from each vineyard is handled separately to preserve its individual character. According to Michael Lee, one of the winery's founders and who is also a wine-maker, such "small lot" winemaking

allows each lot of grapes to be brought to its fullest potential before blending. Likewise, the acclaimed Artist Series is a masterful blend of the top barrels of Cabernet Sauvignon.

The historic barn and other original buildings lend a nostalgic ambience to the modern wine-making facilities on the twenty-two-acre estate. But there is another link to the romantic history of the Valley of the Moon, as author London dubbed Sonoma Valley.

Best known for his rugged individualism and dynamic writing, London was also an accomplished farmer and rancher. At the heart of his Beauty Ranch—now part of the Jack London State Historic Park—several hundred acres of vineyards were planted in the 1870s on terraced slopes. The volcanic ash fields produced excellent wines by the turn of the twentieth century. London died in 1916, and by World War II, his crop fields had become overgrown. But in 1976, Kenwood Vineyards became the exclusive marketer of wines produced from the ranch. The Cabernet Sauvignon, Zinfandel, Merlot, and Pinot Noir, made only from Jack London vineyard grapes, bear a label with the image of a wolf's head, London's signature stamp.

Known for consistency of quality in both its red and its white wines, Kenwood produces mostly moderately priced wines. The major exception is the Artist Series Cabernet Sauvignons, which have been collector's items since first released in 1978.

LANDMARK VINEYARDS

This tidy, twenty-acre estate at the foot of Sugarloaf Mountain represents a melding of the owners' agricultural heritage, the winery's historical architectural style, and a reverence for wine as an integral component of social interaction. At its center is a five-thousand-square-foot courtyard where visitors may mingle, enjoy wines with delicacies from the tasting room, and take in the impressive view of the forested mountain slopes that tower over the town of Kenwood.

Although the winery made its mark initially with two notable Burgundian grapes, Chardonnay and Pinot Noir, it has continued the innovative agricultural traditions of its founding family by adding Rhône varieties such as Syrah, Grenache, Mourvèdre, Syrah, and Counoise, a lesser-known red grape selected for blending purposes. Wine aficionados who are unable to grow their own grapes can  adopt a row of grapevines at Landmark, entitling them to have their name on a plaque in the new vineyards closest to the winery.

Landmark Vineyards was established in 1974 by Damaris Deere Ford. A great-great-granddaughter of John Deere, whose 1838 invention of the steel plow revolutionized the business of agriculture, she had the Spanish mission-style winery built in 1989. With the help of renowned landscape architect Morgan Wheelock, the winery grounds were developed into a lush estate embellished with poplar trees, rosebushes, and flowering vines suspended from the eaves. A tall, graceful fountain is the visual centerpiece of the courtyard.

Michael Deere Colhoun and his wife, Mary Colhoun, continue to expand aspects of the winery's hospitality. Beyond the courtyard, visitors will find an area for lawn games and picnic tables in the shade of a century-old walnut tree. All this and much more can be seen from the President's Tower above the tasting room, the location of private, catered events.

Another view of the property has been captured on canvas by Sonoma County artist Claudia Wagar. Her dramatic mural behind the granite bar in the tasting room is a fanciful rendering of the view from one of Landmark's estate vineyards, progressing from a close-up of a grape cluster to Sugarloaf Mountain in the background. In the tasting room, visitors sample wines from the estate vineyards as well as from a range of other vineyards selected as the finest representatives of California's diverse microclimates. True to the proprietors' focus on family, the wine labels reflect their John Deere heritage: Landmark and Overlook Chardonnays were named for family homes, Grand Detour Pinot Noir recalls the location of the Deeres' original blacksmithing shop in Illinois, and Steel Plow Syrah is aptly named for the invention that made it all possible.

LANDMARK VINEYARDS
101 Adobe Canyon Rd.
Kenwood, CA 95452
707-833-0218
info@landmarkwine.com
www.landmarkwine.com

OWNERS: Mike and Mary Colhoun.

LOCATION: Intersection of Hwy. 12 and Adobe Canyon Rd., approximately midway between Sonoma and Santa Rosa.

APPELLATION: Sonoma Valley.

HOURS: 10 A.M.–4:30 P.M. daily.

TASTINGS: $5 for 3 wines; $10 for 3 reserve wines; $15 for special flight.

TOURS: Vineyard tour and tasting 11 A.M., by appointment ($15).

THE WINES: Chardonnay, Pinot Noir, Syrah.

SPECIALTIES: Chardonnay and single-vineyard wines.

WINEMAKER: Greg Stach.

ANNUAL PRODUCTION: 25,000 cases.

OF SPECIAL NOTE: Guest cottage and suite available for overnight stays. Live music on Saturdays. Horse-drawn wagon rides through vineyards on Saturdays in summer. Picnic fare and seating available. Single-vineyard wines available only in tasting room.

NEARBY ATTRACTIONS: Sugarloaf Ridge State Park (hiking, camping, horseback riding); Annadel State Park (hiking, biking).

LEDSON WINERY & VINEYARDS

LEDSON WINERY & VINEYARDS
7335 Hwy. 12
Kenwood, CA 95409
707-537-3810
www.ledson.com

OWNER: Steve Noble Ledson.

LOCATION: About 2 miles northwest of the town of Kenwood.

APPELLATION: Sonoma Valley.

HOURS: 10 A.M.–5 P.M. daily

TASTINGS: $15 for 6 wines; $20 for 9 wines; $25 for wine consultant picks; $35 for private tasting. Cheese trays available.

TOURS: Self-guided.

THE WINES: Barbera, Cabernet Franc, Cabernet Sauvignon, Carignane, Chardonnay, Grenache, Malbec, Meritage, Merlot, Mourvèdre, Orange Muscat, Petite Sirah, Petit Verdot, Pinot Noir, Port, Riesling, Sangiovese, Sauvignon Blanc, Syrah, Zinfandel.

SPECIALTIES: Small lots of handcrafted Cabernet Sauvignon, Chardonnay, Merlot, Sauvignon Blanc, Zinfandel.

WINEMAKER: Steve Noble Ledson.

ANNUAL PRODUCTION: 35,000 cases.

OF SPECIAL NOTE: Wines only available at winery, hotel, and online. Gourmet Marketplace offers a variety of foods. Ledson Hotel & Harmony Lounge, a 6-room hotel and wine bar, located on Sonoma Plaza.

NEARBY ATTRACTION: Annadel State Park (hiking, biking).

It came to be known widely as "The Castle"—some people say it reminds them of a French castle in Normandy. The architectural showpiece took ten years and some two million bricks to build. When the Ledson family started construction in 1992, they thought the property would be ideal for their residence. They planted Merlot vineyards and began work on the house. As the months passed, the turrets, slate roofs, balconies, and fountains took shape, and passersby would even climb over the fence to get a better look.

Steve Ledson finally realized it was time to rethink his plan. Given the intense public interest in the building and the quality of the grape harvests—which were sold to nearby wineries—he decided to turn the sixteen-thousand-square-foot structure into a winery and tasting room. In 1997 he released the winery's first wine: the 1994 Estate Merlot. After two years of reconstruction, the winery opened in 1999.

Fortunately, Ledson not only had his own construction company but also benefited from his family's history of farming in the area, beginning in the 1860s. His great-great-grandfather on his father's side was an early pioneer in Sonoma County winemaking, and both sets of grandparents had worked adjoining Sonoma Valley ranches cooperatively. Eventually, this Ledson acreage became part of the Annadel State Park. The family had grown grapes for years, so Steve, the fifth generation to farm in the area, jumped at the chance to buy the twenty-one-acre property to plant Estate Merlot. The property just happened to have a view of Annadel State Park.

Visitors to The Castle find an estate worthy of the French countryside, with a grand brick driveway, a manicured landscape, and a flourishing collection of roses. Just inside the front door is a grand staircase that reminds people of the movie *Gone with the Wind*. The Castle has more than five miles of ceiling moldings and sixteen thousand square feet of hardwood flooring spread over four floors of twenty-seven rooms, each with a different pattern of wood inlays. Twelve rooms are visible to the public: nine tasting rooms, a gourmet marketplace, a parlor area, and a club room.

At Ledson, visitors are treated to a sensory feast. The Gourmet Marketplace features a tempting selection of gourmet meats, artisan cheeses, fresh made-to-order sandwiches, salads, and desserts, as well as an extensive selection of locally produced gourmet items, including olive oils. Guests can enjoy a picnic lunch outdoors at tables overlooking the estate vineyards and fountains, or in The Castle's intimate parlor with its elegant Italian marble fireplaces and breathtaking views.

MARTINELLI WINERY

The bright red hop barn sitting only a few yards off River Road is a photo opportunity waiting to happen. The tasting room entrance is a sheltered nook where wooden tables and benches, gracefully weathered to a soft gray, sit beneath a vine-covered trellis. Beyond the barn, rows of vineyards march up a hill, interspersed with a trio of arbors perfect for picnicking.

The scene could well be the setting for an old-fashioned movie romanticizing rural life, but the Martinelli Winery is the real thing. The Martinelli family has been growing grapes in the Russian River Valley since 1887, and successive generations have kept their immigrant ancestors' dreams alive over the decades.

At the tender ages of nineteen and sixteen, Giuseppe Martinelli and Luisa Vellutini eloped from their village in the  Tuscany region of Italy, bound for California in search of land where they could start a winery. Giuseppe had been a winemaker in Italy, and with his knowledge of viticulture, he was hired by a local farmer to work in a vineyard in Forestville. Within two years, the hardworking young man was able to purchase some land. Giuseppe and Luisa, working side by side on a sixty-degree slope, planted Zinfandel and Muscat Alexandria vines on what would eventually become known as the Jackass Hill vineyard. Luisa's uphill struggle was just beginning. Giuseppe died in 1918, leaving his widow with four children and a farm to run. The youngest Martinelli son, Leno, left school after the eighth grade and began farming the Zinfandel vineyard all by himself. How did the vineyard get its name? Leno's family told him that only a jackass would farm a hill that steep.

Armed with his parents' knowledge and his own experience, Leno persevered, even using a horse and plow to work the land until 1949, when he finally bought a tractor. Only at the age of eighty-nine did he finally hang up the keys to his John Deere and relinquish the reins to his son, Lee. In 1973 Lee took over management of his uncle Tony Bondi's adjacent estate, located minutes away from Jackass Hill, and planted vineyards where apple orchards once flourished.

When Lee and his wife, Carolyn, decided to start a winery on the property, they converted a pair of hop barns into the winemaking facility and tasting room, taking care to preserve the historic character of the buildings. Today, Lee Sr. and his two sons, Lee Jr. and George, do all the farming. References to the Martinelli farming heritage are visible in the cozy tasting room store, where, amid rustic hutches stocked with linens and unique gifts, ancient winery equipment and faded family photographs are on display.

MARTINELLI WINERY
3360 River Rd.
Windsor, CA 95492
800-346-1627
vinoinfo@
martinelliwinery.com
www.martinelliwinery.com

OWNERS: Lee Sr. and Carolyn Martinelli and their 4 children.

LOCATION: About 2 miles west of U.S. 101 via River Rd./Mark West Springs Rd. exit.

APPELLATION: Russian River Valley.

HOURS: 10 A.M.–5 P.M. daily.

TASTINGS: $5.

TOURS: By appointment.

THE WINES: Chardonnay, Muscat Alexandria, Pinot Noir, Syrah, Zinfandel.

SPECIALTIES: Wines made from estate-grown grapes.

WINEMAKERS: Helen Turley, consulting winemaker; Bryan Kvamme, winemaker.

ANNUAL PRODUCTION: 10,000 cases.

OF SPECIAL NOTE: All wines are made from estate grapes and are 100 percent varietal. Several picnic tables with vineyard views scattered throughout the property.

NEARBY ATTRACTIONS: Wells Fargo Center for the Performing Arts; Russian River (rafting, fishing, swimming, canoeing, kayaking).

MATANZAS CREEK WINERY

MATANZAS CREEK WINERY
6097 Bennett Valley Rd.
Santa Rosa, CA 95404
707-528-6464
800-590-6464
info@matanzascreek.com
www.matanzascreek.com

OWNERS: Jess Jackson and
Barbara Banke.

LOCATION: About 6 miles
southeast of Santa Rosa.

APPELLATIONS: Bennett
Valley, Sonoma Valley.

HOURS: 10 A.M.–4:30 P.M.
daily.

TASTINGS: $5 for 4 or
5 wines.

TOURS: By appointment,
10:30 A.M. and 2:30 P.M.
Monday–Friday and
10:30 A.M. Saturday.

THE WINES: Cabernet
Sauvignon, Chardonnay,
Merlot, Pinot Noir, Rosé,
Sauvignon Blanc, Syrah.

SPECIALTIES: Chardonnay,
Merlot, Sauvignon Blanc.

WINEMAKER:
François Cordesse.

ANNUAL PRODUCTION:
40,000–45,000 cases.

OF SPECIAL NOTE: Extensive
garden. Picnic area beneath
oak trees with vineyard
views. Gift shop featuring
soap, sachets, grilling
sticks, and other items
made from estate-grown
lavender. Jackson Park
Merlot, Rosé, and Ultime
(red dessert wine) available
only at winery.

NEARBY ATTRACTIONS:
Luther Burbank Garden
and Home (tours of famed
horticulturist's property);
Charles M. Schulz Museum
(exhibits on *Peanuts* creator
and other cartoonists).

Matanzas Creek Winery presides over the picturesque Bennett Valley, one of the most serene and unspoiled of all California's winegrowing regions. Located between Sonoma Valley and the city of Santa Rosa, the winery enjoys the best of both worlds: it is well off the beaten path yet easily accessed from several directions.

Founded in 1977 on the site of a former dairy farm, the original winery was replaced in 1985 with a modern winemaking demand for its Chardonnay addition to the complex is a built in 2000. Over the past Winery's vineyard holdings have Merlot and Syrah added in the total estate plantings to more of the 120-acre Jackson Park facility to accommodate growing and Merlot. The most recent barrel chai, a barrel-aging facility, three decades, Matanzas Creek doubled in size. New plantings of late 1990s increased the winery's than 80 acres. The development Vineyard (located across Bennett Valley Road from the winery) in 1996 cemented Matanzas Creek Winery's leadership role in the Bennett Valley winegrowing community.

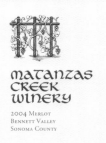

MATANZAS CREEK WINERY
2004 MERLOT
BENNETT VALLEY
SONOMA COUNTY

Surrounded by Taylor Mountain to the west, Sonoma Mountain to the south, and Bennett Peak to the east, the valley is cooled by coastal fog and breezes that drift northeast through the Crane Canyon gap and provide a long growing season that gives the grapes complex characteristics. The vines also benefit from a diversity of soil types, including deposits of ash on the valley floor from the surrounding volcanic peaks, as well as basalt, an ancient ocean-floor rock that imparts a slightly smoky character to the Matanzas Creek Merlot.

Matanzas Creek Winery began capitalizing on these attributes nearly three decades before Bennett Valley was recognized as an American Viticultural Area (AVA), one of the newest in Sonoma County. At one time defined as part of the county's Sonoma Valley and Sonoma Mountain AVAs, Bennett Valley overlaps with these regions but also carves out 8,150 acres to call its own. The appellation was formalized in 2003, although Bennett Valley's hospitable grape-growing environment was first discovered as early as the mid-1800s.

The winery was named after a nearby stream called Matanzas by the early Spanish for the Pomo Indian deer hunts that were once common in the area. It remains one of the few tasting rooms in the entire valley. Visitors are entranced with the winery's extravagant, terraced perennial gardens and its trademark one-acre plot of aromatic lavender. They can shop for souvenirs of the estate's lavender garden, including bath, beauty, home décor, and culinary products.

MERRIAM VINEYARDS

When Peter and Diana Merriam wed in 1982, they honeymooned among the vineyards of France. The trip ignited a passion for wine, and in 1988 the New England natives bought a wine shop near Boston. They frequently traveled to France on business and to immerse themselves in the country's culture of food and wine. Eager to start a winery and promote that culture at home, the couple began searching for vineyard property in 1995. They understood that quality grapes are required to produce fine wine and hoped to buy an established vineyard boasting pedigreed fruit. They sought advice from an old friend from Maine, Tom Simoneau, a winemaker and radio personality who had moved  to Sonoma County and planted his own vineyard in 1988. With his help, they found the eleven-acre Windacre Vineyard, near Healdsburg. In 2000 the couple purchased the property, which had originally been planted to wine grapes in 1890. Located in the warmest corner of the Russian River Valley appellation, the vineyard was replanted in 2003 with Bordeaux varieties.

The Merriams blended their first vintage of California-style Bordeaux in 2000, three years before finding ideal acreage for the winery on the east side of the Russian River. It took six years to secure permits and finish construction, and in 2009 the winery and tasting room opened. That same year, the couple planted a second estate vineyard to Pinot Noir, Sauvignon Blanc, and Semillon on eight acres surrounding the winery. The vineyard is expected to be certified organic by 2012. The winery supplements estate fruit by purchasing Cabernet Sauvignon from Passalacqua Vineyard, a Dry Creek Valley site with late-ripening grapes, and Dunnsden Vineyard, in Russian River Valley. Cabernet Franc is sourced from Jones Vineyard, in Dry Creek Valley, and Chardonnay comes from Simoneau, who also sells fruit to Windsor Wines.

The winery and tasting room stand on a low hill with views of rolling vineyards and coastal ridges to the west. Steeply pitched roofs and wide covered porches give the structures a New England flavor. Inside, the tasting room resembles a spacious farmhouse, complete with hand-hewn oak floors and an old table with a traditional soapstone top. Antique furnishings include a bottle corker, a carpenter's bench, and harvest baskets, as well as a polished wooden bench that serves as a window seat.

Several of the wines are served with small bites prepared on-site. Pairings include crostini with artisanal cheese, pâté, and chocolate, depending on the wine poured. The Merriams, who divide their time between New England and Sonoma County, sell 60 percent of their wine to restaurants and retailers back east, reserving most of the other 40 percent for the tasting room.

MERRIAM VINEYARDS
11650 Los Amigos Rd.
Healdsburg, CA 95448
707-433-4032
info@merriamvineyards.com
www.merriamvineyards.com

OWNERS: Peter and Diana Merriam.

LOCATION: 3.5 miles south of Healdsburg.

APPELLATION: Russian River Valley.

HOURS: 10 A.M.–5 P.M. daily.

TASTINGS: Complimentary for Signature wines. $10 for reserve wines includes small bite pairings. Fee refunded with wine purchase. $20 for 8 wines paired with crackers and 4 different cheeses, by appointment.

TOURS: Complimentary tours by appointment made 24 hours in advance.

THE WINES: Cabernet Franc, Cabernet Sauvignon, Chardonnay, Merlot, Petit Verdot.

SPECIALTIES: Red Bordeaux blends, Miktos (red Bordeaux blend).

WINEMAKER: Margaret Davenport.

ANNUAL PRODUCTION: 2,500 cases

OF SPECIAL NOTE: Library wines tasted on rotating basis. Fine art and photographs by local artists for sale in tasting room. New England lobster bake held in July, Harvest Dinner in October.

NEARBY ATTRACTION: Russian River (swimming, canoeing, kayaking, rafting, fishing).

SBRAGIA FAMILY VINEYARDS

SBRAGIA FAMILY VINEYARDS
9990 Dry Creek Rd.
Geyserville, CA 95441
707-473-2992
info@sbragia.com
www.sbragia.com

OWNERS: Ed Sbragia and
Jane Sbragia.

LOCATION: 10 miles
northwest of Healdsburg.

APPELLATION: Dry Creek
Valley.

HOURS: 11 A.M.–5 P.M. daily.

TASTINGS: $5 for 3 or
4 wines for standard
tasting; $10 for 3 or
4 wines for reserve
tasting. Ark tastings
by appointment.

TOURS: By appointment
only ($15 per person).

THE WINES: Cabernet
Sauvignon, Chardonnay,
Merlot, Sauvignon Blanc,
Zinfandel.

SPECIALTIES: Cabernet
Sauvignon, Chardonnay,
Zinfandel.

WINEMAKERS: Ed Sbragia,
Adam Sbragia.

ANNUAL PRODUCTION:
8,500 cases.

OF SPECIAL NOTE: Winery
specializes in single-
vineyard wines. Tables
and chairs for picnicking
on an expansive terrace
with views of the Dry
Creek Valley. Gift shop.
Some prepared foods sold
at winery. Annual events
include Barrel Tasting
(March) and Passport
Weekend (April).

NEARBY ATTRACTION:
Lake Sonoma (swimming,
fishing, boating, camping,
hiking).

Just before Dry Creek Road reaches its western terminus at Lake Sonoma, the Sbragia Family Vineyards winery, perched on a hill, comes into view. Visitors approach the winery on a winding driveway that passes through Zinfandel vineyards and lush gardens. Among the features they first see is the generous terrace overlooking the vineyards. The setting is an ideal one for an afternoon of tasting and enjoying the vista from the top of Dry Creek Valley, an impressive panorama that takes in Mount St. Helena on the eastern horizon.

Sbragia Family Vineyards is many miles from the place where Ed Sbragia gained acclaim during his thirty years of making award-winning wines at Beringer Vine- yards in Napa Valley before retiring in 2008. Seven years before he left Beringer, he had started producing wine under the Sbragia Family Vineyards label. As reflected in the winery's name, the business is a family affair. Ed Sbragia shares cellar duties with his son, Adam. Adam's wife, Kathy, is in charge of hospitality for the winery, and Ed's wife, Jane, and daughter, Gina, are often found behind the tasting bar.

The family's roots grow deepest in this part of Sonoma County. After purchasing land in Dry Creek Valley, the Sbragias grew and dried plums there for years. By the early 1960s, Ed's father, Gino Sbragia, had planted grapevines, which Ed helped tend until he went off to study chemistry at the University of California, Davis, and then earn an enology degree at Fresno State. Gino Sbragia, who died in 1995, had tried to start a winery, but Prohibition and the Great Depression prevented him from realizing his dream. Ed Sbragia promised his father that he would eventually establish a winery of his own. Among other endeavors, the family had run a restaurant and bar called the Ark. That name is honored today as a private reserve tasting room at the winery.

Ed and Adam Sbragia's focus is on making vineyard-designated wines. Five—Chardonnay, Sauvignon Blanc, Merlot, and two Zinfandels—are grown on estate vineyards. A vineyard owned by Ed's uncle provides fruit for another Zinfandel. Chardonnay is also sourced from one of Ed's favorite vineyards, Gamble Ranch in Napa Valley. Fruit for five Sbragia Cabernet Sauvignons comes from various mountain-top vineyards: Andolsen Vineyard in Dry Creek Valley, Monte Rosso Vineyards in Sonoma's Mayacamas Range, Wall Vineyard on Mount Veeder in Napa, and Rancho Del Oso and Cimarossa Vineyard on Napa's Howell Mountain. Of the estate vineyards, two are named in honor of Gino Sbragia. Gino's Vineyard was planted to Zinfandel more than two decades ago. La Promessa Vineyard, also producing Zinfandel, acknowledges Ed's fulfilled promise to his father.

SEBASTIANI VINEYARDS AND WINERY

Sebastiani Vineyards has prospered for more than a hundred years on a quiet street in the town of Sonoma. One of California's oldest, continuously operated wineries, it stands just a few hundred feet from the site of Sonoma Valley's first vineyard, planted in 1825 by Franciscan fathers. The basalt block walls of the original winery—built in 1903—are visible from the street and incorporated into the hospitality center. A circular fountain fills the courtyard with sparkling motion, and a Romanesque arcade runs the length of the building, shading bistro tables grouped along the front.

Arched wooden doors with wrought iron grills open to reveal a cathedral-like interior that hints at founder Samuele Sebastiani's wine-making apprenticeship in an Italian monastery. Ceiling vaults supported by Tuscan columns glow in soft light. A gently curving tasting bar extends eighty feet, and an assortment of stools and leather chairs invites guests to linger over their glasses of wine.

Visitors can join a "Soil to Bottle" tour that departs three times daily or can set their own pace on a self-guided stroll through the winery's museum of Sebastiani family mementos. The first stop showcases a massive, 60,000-gallon oak tank that was milled in Germany and assembled at the winery more than a hundred years ago. Used for making Zinfandel until 1989, it, along with a twin in Heidelberg, are the only two that exist in the world. A glance upward reveals what remains of a third, its polished staves now part of the ceiling. Nearby stands Samuele's wooden crusher and his first 500-gallon barrel, the same one he loaded onto a wagon when he began selling wine door to door in 1904. In the adjacent Sonoma Lounge, an entire wall bears a colorful fresco of the Sonoma area as it looked early in the twentieth century.

The Sebastiani legacy also boasts the largest collection of hand-carved wine barrels in the United States, many of them on display here. Earle Brown, a master woodcarver affectionately dubbed the "human termite," worked for August Sebastiani, Samuele's son, from 1967 to 1984, adorning doors, barrels, and plaques with carved images of wine-related scenes.

In December 2008, Bill Foley purchased Sebastiani Winery, and he continues to run it as a family business. Winemaster Mark Lyons, who has been with the winery for thirty years, remains at his post and still makes all the wine on-site.

On summer weekends, locals and visitors wander the wide lawns and sit under wisteria-draped arbors enjoying wine, art, food, and live music.

SEBASTIANI VINEYARDS AND WINERY
389 Fourth St. East
Sonoma, CA 95476
707-933-3200
800-888-5532, ext. 3230
info@sebastiani.com
www.sebastiani.com

OWNER: Bill Foley.

LOCATION: 3 blocks east of the historic Sonoma Square via E. Spain St.

APPELLATION: Sonoma Valley.

HOURS: 10 A.M.–5 P.M. daily.

TASTINGS: $10 for standard tasting of 7 wines; $15 for reserve tasting of 7 wines. Reservations required for groups of 8 or more.

TOURS: 11 A.M., 1 P.M., and 3 P.M. daily.

THE WINES: Barbera, Cabernet Sauvignon, Chardonnay, Merlot, Pinot Noir, Roussanne, Syrah, Zinfandel.

SPECIALTIES: Alexander Valley Cabernet Sauvignon and Chardonnay, Carneros Chardonnay, Dry Creek Zinfandel.

WINEMAKER: Mark Lyons.

ANNUAL PRODUCTION: 220,000 cases.

OF SPECIAL NOTE: Winery is at eastern end of Sonoma City Trail, a dedicated bike path. Large, sycamore-shaded picnic area with vineyard views is located along Lovall Valley Rd. Live music on Friday nights, May–December. Barbecue dinners on summer weekends. Food-and-wine pairings by appointment ($25–$30). Extensive gift shop.

NEARBY ATTRACTIONS: Mission San Francisco Solano and other historic buildings in downtown Sonoma; bike rentals.

SIDURI WINES

SIDURI WINES
981 Airway Ct.,
Suites E and F
Santa Rosa, CA 95403
707-578-3882
pinot@siduri.com
www.siduri.com
www.novyfamilywines.
com

OWNERS: Adam and
Dianna Lee.

LOCATION: Off Airway Ct.
between Industrial Dr. and
Piner Rd., about .5 mile
west of U.S. 101.

APPELLATIONS: Various in
Oregon and California.

HOURS: By appointment.
10 A.M.–3 P.M. daily.

TASTINGS: Complimentary
for 6–8 wines.

TOURS: Included with
tasting.

THE WINES: Chardonnay,
Grenache, Nebbiolo, Pinot
Meunier, Pinot Noir,
Syrah, Viognier, Zinfandel.

SPECIALTIES: Single-
vineyard Pinot Noir
and Syrah.

WINEMAKERS: Adam and
Dianna Lee.

ANNUAL PRODUCTION:
12,000 cases.

OF SPECIAL NOTE: Annual
events include Barrel
Tasting (March) and Open
Houses (summer and
winter).

NEARBY ATTRACTIONS:
Charles M. Schulz
Museum (exhibits on
Peanuts creator and other
cartoonists); Sonoma
County Museum (regional
history and contemporary
art and culture); Pacific
Coast Air Museum; Luther
Burbank Garden and
Home (tours of famed
horticulturist's property).

This is no-frills wine tasting at its best. Not only are there no sweeping driveways, grand architectural statements, or lavishly landscaped grounds, but there are virtually no signs directing drivers to Siduri. Hidden in a cul-de-sac in a neighborhood better known for chain stores and discount furniture outlets, the entrance is so low-key that first-time visitors might think they have to whisper a password to get in. Hardly, but they do need an appointment. Once inside the building, they won't have to wait in line or share the attention of the staff with a crowd of drop-ins.

Siduri's location in a warehouse may seem odd for a winery, but it fits the philosophy of its founders. Adam and Dianna Lee met in Dallas, where both were working for Neiman-Marcus—he as a wine buyer, she in the epicurean department. Native Texans and self-described wine geeks, they soon discovered their mutual love of Pinot Noir, especially those made in Sonoma by Tom Rochioli and Williams Selyem, two of the most notable Pinot producers of the last twenty-five years. They also shared a simple ambition: to move to California and "make killer Pinot Noir from the finest vineyards" they could find.

They established Siduri in 1994, naming it for the Babylonian goddess of wine who, according to myth and legend, held the wine of eternal life. With a conviction as big as the Texas sky, they figured they would learn winemaking as they went along. After they moved to California and got married, the Lees both worked at a number of small, family-owned wineries, which was a natural fit.

Believing that the best wines in the world come from low-yielding grapevines, Adam and Dianna Lee buy grapes by the acre rather than by the ton, so that growers can focus on low yields rather than high tonnage. The first Siduri release was 107 cases of 1994 Anderson Valley Pinot Noir Rose Vineyard. In the early days, the Lees made their wine at Lambert Bridge Winery in Dry Creek Valley, before establishing their own facility in 1998. Guided by the principle of concentrating on single-vineyard wines that reflect the personality of those sites, the Lees buy grapes from dozens of vineyards up and down the West Coast, from Oregon's Willamette Valley south to the Santa Rita Hills in Santa Barbara County.

There is something so intense about loving Pinot Noir that the varietal's most passionate fans are known as Pinot Noiristes. It is not surprising, then, that the vibe inside Siduri is akin to that of a secret club. At the appointed hour, visitors gather in front of a canyon of oak barrels in the "tasting room," where dozens of bottles are displayed atop upended wine barrels. The session also features wines from Novy Family Winery, which is owned by the Lees and Dianna's parents, brothers, and sisters-in-law.

SILVER OAK CELLARS

A Tudor-style estate set at the top of a lawn-covered slope, Silver Oak Cellars in Geyserville specializes in Alexander Valley Cabernet Sauvignon. Although unusual, this commitment to a single variety and appellation has succeeded, for Silver Oak wines are recognized worldwide for their elegance and complexity.

Winemaker Daniel Baron sources fruit from estate vineyards growing beside the winery, as well as from select Alexander Valley growers. To enhance the opulent, well-rounded flavors, Baron barrel-ages the wine for two years. Instead of using French oak barrels, he prefers American oak because it imparts softer tannins, more vanilla components, and fresh spicy notes. To ensure a supply of barrels that meet Silver Oak's standards, the winery has contracted with a Midwest-based cooper to purchase several hundred acres of white oak timberland in Missouri. The wood is harvested when ready and made into barrels according to Baron's specifications.

The winery's use of American oak barrels began with the late Justin Meyer, who cofounded Silver Oak Cellars in Oakville in 1972. A former Christian Brothers wine-maker, Meyer felt that the tannins in French oak were too harsh for his Alexander Valley fruit. Meyer's business partner was Ray Duncan, a Colorado entrepreneur drawn to California in the 1960s. Sensing the region's potential for wine, Duncan eventually purchased 750 acres of land in Napa and Alexander valleys.

When Duncan proposed they start a winery, Meyer agreed, and the visionary vintners proceeded to make history with their singular Cabernet Sauvignon. Meyer crafted all of the wine at the Oakville winery until 1993, when the pair opened the sister estate in Geyserville as the exclusive producer of Silver Oak's Alexander Valley Cabernet Sauvignon. Vintages from the two properties remain distinctly different. The somewhat bolder Napa Valley wines from the Oakville estate boast firm tannins, while the Geyserville wines display soft, fruity characteristics. Visitors tasting at the Geyserville estate pass through arched glass doors into the spacious tasting room. The tasting bar—built from milled oak and accented with steel strips—suggests, appropriately, an American oak barrel. During the early 1990s, Silver Oak began hosting semiannual parties for the release of the wines from each estate. Both estates offer a festive day of food, wine tasting, and, perhaps best of all, the chance to take home bottles of coveted Cabernet Sauvignon. Since 2001, after acquiring Meyer's share of the wineries, the Duncan family has continued to helm Silver Oak Cellars with their trademark commitment to quality Cabernet Sauvignon.

SILVER OAK CELLARS
24625 Chianti Rd.
Geyserville, CA 95441
707-942-7082
800-273-8809
info@silveroak.com
www.silveroak.com

OWNERS: Duncan family.

LOCATION: 3 miles north of Geyserville.

APPELLATION: Alexander Valley.

HOURS: 9 A.M.–5 P.M. Monday–Saturday, 11 A.M.–5 P.M. Sunday, in summer; 9 A.M.–4 P.M. Monday–Saturday, 11 A.M.–4 P.M. Sunday, in winter.

TASTINGS: $10 for current releases (complimentary glass included). Reservations suggested for groups of 8 or more.

TOURS: The Silver Tour and Taste ($10), offering tour of winery and tasting of current vintages. Monday–Friday, 1:30 P.M., by reservation.

THE WINE: Cabernet Sauvignon.

SPECIALTY: Cabernet Sauvignon.

WINEMAKER: Daniel Baron.

ANNUAL PRODUCTION: 70,000 cases.

OF SPECIAL NOTE: Release Day is held simultaneously at both estates for each wine: Napa Valley Cabernet on the first Saturday in February; Alexander Valley Cabernet on the first Saturday in August. Purchase limits on some vintages.

NEARBY ATTRACTION: Lake Sonoma (swimming, fishing, boating, camping, hiking).

St. Francis Winery & Vineyards

St. Francis Winery & Vineyards
100 Pythian Rd.
(at Hwy. 12)
Santa Rosa, CA 95409
888-675-WINE (9463)
info@stfranciswinery.com
www.stfranciswinery.com

President and CEO:
Christopher Silva.

Location: Off Hwy. 12, 6 miles east of Santa Rosa and 1 mile west of the town of Kenwood.

Appellation: Sonoma Valley.

Hours: 10 A.M.–5 P.M. daily.

Tastings: $10–$15 for 4 wines; $35 for 4 wines paired with food.

Tours: "Wine-cation" production tours offered twice daily on weekends. Reservations recommended.

The Wines: Cabernet Franc, Cabernet Sauvignon, Chardonnay, Claret, Malbec, Mourvèdre, Merlot, Petite Sirah, Port, Rosé, Sauvignon Blanc, Syrah, Viognier, Zinfandel.

Specialty: 100 percent handpicked Sonoma County grapes.

Winemaker: Tom Mackey.

Annual Production: 250,000 cases.

Of Special Note: Daily extensive wine-and-food pairings. Winery dinners and educational events listed online. Annual events include Barrel Tasting (March) and Blessing of the Animals (fall).

Nearby Attractions: Sugarloaf Ridge State Park (hiking, camping, horseback riding); Annadel State Park (hiking, biking).

If St. Francis Winery & Vineyards wanted a catchy commercial come-on, it might be: Come for the wine, stay for the food. The winery was one of the first in California to offer an extensive wine-and-food-pairing program and has never lost its leading edge. Executive chef Dave Bush is on staff to create innovative dishes to complement the winery's many food-friendly varietals.

The culinary focus began shortly after St. Francis relocated one mile north of its modest origins to a brand-new facility in 2001. Built in the style of the early California missions, the red-tile-roofed, sand-colored stucco hospitality center is sited at the entrance of the vener- able Wild Oak Vineyard, with Hood Mountain as a backdrop. A tower near the tasting room features a bell that is rung to mark every hour. According to a plaque displayed on one side of the tower, the bell was cast by a historic Italian foundry and blessed in the Piazza della Basilica of St. Francis of Assisi.

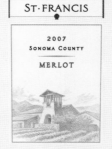

Forty years ago, long before the wine world began to recognize the Sonoma County *terroir* as among the finest in the world, St. Francis Winery made the commitment to craft wines exclusively from Sonoma. The winery owns more than six hundred estate acres of prime vineyards in Sonoma Valley and Russian River Valley. Under the direction of winemaker Tom Mackey, each vineyard was planted row by row, block by block, with varietals particularly well suited to each site. St. Francis now reaps the rewards through a bounty of outstanding fruit from superior mountain and valley vineyards in Sonoma County's best appellations.

The first stop for most visitors is the tasting room, where the beamed ceiling soars over twenty feet, and warmth is provided by wood paneling—and, in winter, by a roaring fireplace. Tasting is available inside or out on the patio. There, umbrellas shade wooden tables and chairs arranged to create the best vista of the lawns, gardens, and Hood Mountain.

The Sonoma Valley's mild climate allows for being outdoors most of the year, especially from May through October. That time frame coincides with the winery's Wine and Charcuterie Pairing Program. Seated outside on a shaded patio, guests are served flights of red or white wines along with a selection of artisan meats and cheeses. Throughout the year, they can gather indoors at a commu-nal table to enjoy a menu of small plates prepared by the winery's chef. The offerings are changed seasonally to reflect the freshest local products available. The artfully prepared dishes are created to compliment four estate wines poured at each sitting. One menu might partner Syrah-braised pork cheeks and a glass of Wild Oak Syrah, or roasted *merguez* meatball and sautéed ratatouille and a Dry Creek Valley Petite Sirah.

TWOMEY CELLARS

Twomey Cellars was founded in Calistoga in 1999 by the Duncan family of Silver Oak Cellars with the purpose of producing Merlot from the family's Soda Canyon Ranch in Napa. In the cellar, Daniel Baron, director of winemaking, uses a rare technique called *soutirage tradicional* to slowly rack the wine from barrel to barrel using gravity and air pressure only. This method yields brilliantly clear wines with lively aromatics and soft tannins.

In 2000 the Duncans broadened their focus to include two other varieties: Pinot Noir and Sauvignon Blanc. They acquired the West Valley of Sonoma County, a region and they began making Sauvignon vineyard in Calistoga.

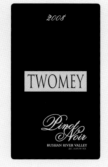

Pin Vineyard in the Russian River noted for its outstanding Pinot Noir, Blanc from their twelve-acre estate

In 2007 the Duncan family (pronounced "TOO-mee") just west Here winemaker Ben Cane crafts Pinot Noir that epitomizes the *terroir* One is Russian River Valley, where the opened a second Twomey Cellars of Healdsburg in Sonoma County. vineyard-driven, regionally based of four select California appellations. Duncans farm the nine-acre West Pin Vineyard. Another is Anderson Valley, the northernmost Pacific Coast valley warm enough to ripen wine grapes, and the site of Monument Tree Vineyard, purchased by the Duncans in 2010. Twomey Cellars sources Pinot Noir from several Sonoma Coast vineyards featuring diverse soils and exposures that yield fruit with equally diverse flavor profiles. To complete the portfolio of regional Pinot Noir, the winery uses fruit solely from the highly acclaimed Bien Nacido Vineyard for its Santa Barbara County Pinot Noir. The vineyard's location ensures that morning fog fosters slow, even ripening of the temperamental Burgundian grape.

Dramatic and light filled, Twomey Cellars' Healdsburg tasting room is a postmodern masterpiece of curving metal rooflines and soft stucco exteriors. A seven-foot-tall arc of concrete forms a welcoming water wall just outside the double glass doors. Designed by Sausalito-based architect Jacques Ullman, the winery won an American Institute of Architects design award in 2004. The tasting room has a poured concrete bar, and windows afford panoramic views of the Coast Range—including 3,455-foot Geyser Peak in Sonoma County and 4,400-foot Mount St. Helena, the Bay Area's tallest peak, located in Napa County. Sharp-eyed observers may also spot towers marking geothermal plants in the distant hills of Lake County. The wrap-around patio borders a lush lawn and is set with glass-topped tables, wicker chairs, and wooden benches, ideal spots for a picnic lunch.

TWOMEY CELLARS
3000 Westside Rd.
Healdsburg, CA 95448
707-942-7150
800-505-4850
info@twomeycellars.com
www.twomeycellars.com

OWNERS: Duncan family.

LOCATION: 2 miles southwest of Healdsburg.

APPELLATION: Russian River Valley.

HOURS: 9 A.M.–5 P.M. Monday–Saturday, 11 A.M.–5 P.M. Sunday, in summer; 9 A.M.–4 P.M. Monday–Saturday, 11 A.M.–4 P.M. Sunday, in winter.

TASTINGS: $10 for 4 wines (includes complimentary glass).

TOURS: By appointment; included in tasting fee.

THE WINES: Merlot, Pinot Noir, Sauvignon Blanc.

SPECIALTY: Pinot Noir.

WINEMAKER: Ben Cane.

ANNUAL PRODUCTION: 15,000 cases.

OF SPECIAL NOTE: Picnic area available. Award-winning architecture.

NEARBY ATTRACTION: Russian River (rafting, fishing, swimming, canoeing, kayaking).

MENDOCINO

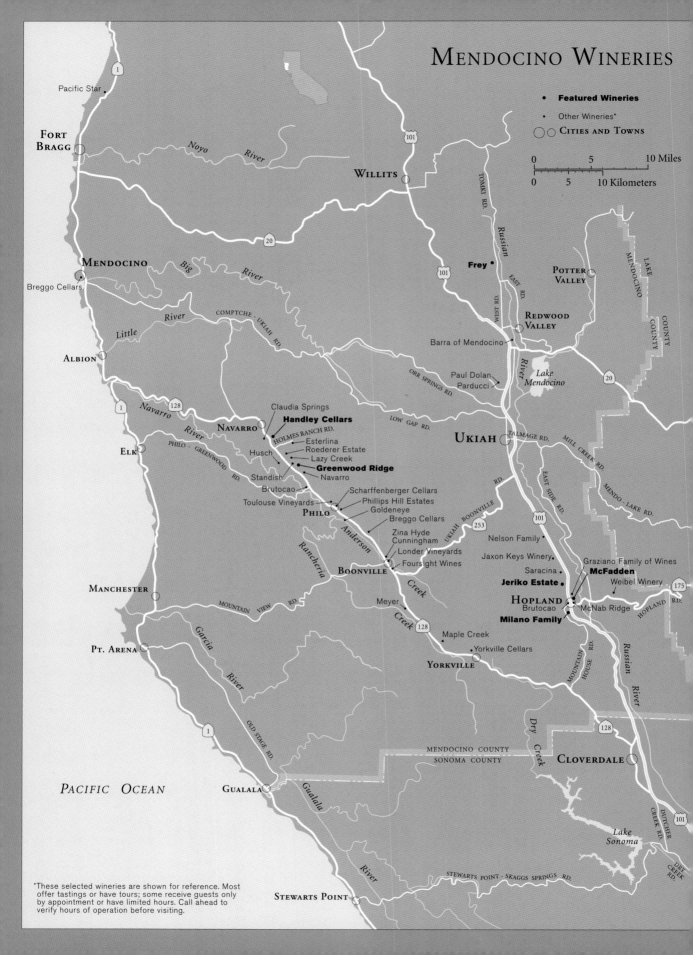

MENDOCINO WINERIES

- ● **Featured Wineries**
- ● Other Wineries*
- ◯ CITIES AND TOWNS

```
0          5        10 Miles
0      5        10 Kilometers
```

FORT BRAGG

Pacific Star ●

Noyo River

WILLITS

101

TOMKI RD.

Frey ●

Russian

POTTER VALLEY

MENDOCINO

Breggo Cellars

Big River

River

Little

EAST RD.

WEST RD.

REDWOOD VALLEY

20

MENDOCINO COUNTY

LAKE COUNTY

COMPTCHE - UKIAH RD.

Barra of Mendocino

ALBION

River

1

128

Navarro River

Paul Dolan
Parducci ●

ORR SPRINGS RD.

Lake Mendocino

River

20

Claudia Springs
Handley Cellars ●

LOW GAP RD.

UKIAH

TALMAGE RD.

MILL CREEK RD.

MENDO - LAKE RD.

NAVARRO

HOLMES RANCH RD.

● Esterlina
● Roederer Estate

Husch

● Lazy Creek

Greenwood Ridge ●

● Navarro

ELK

PHILO - GREENWOOD RD.

Standish

Brutocao

Scharffenberger Cellars

RD.

Phillips Hill Estates

EAST SIDE RD.

101

Toulouse Vineyards

Goldeneye

PHILO

Breggo Cellars

Anderson

Zina Hyde
Cunningham

UKIAH BOONVILLE

253

Nelson Family ●

Londer Vineyards

Jaxon Keys Winery ●

Graziano Family of Wines

Rancheria

Foursight Wines

Saracina ●

McFadden

BOONVILLE

Creek

Jeriko Estate ●

Weibel Winery

HOPLAND

MANCHESTER

MOUNTAIN VIEW RD.

Meyer

Creek

Milano Family

Brutocao

McNab Ridge

175

HOPLAND RD.

PT. ARENA

Garcia

128

Maple Creek ●

MOUNTAIN HOUSE RD.

Russian River

River

OLD STAGE RD.

1

Yorkville Cellars ●

YORKVILLE

Dry Creek

128

MENDOCINO COUNTY

SONOMA COUNTY

CLOVERDALE

PACIFIC OCEAN

GUALALA

Gualala

River

Lake Sonoma

DUTCHER CREEK RD.

101

DRY CREEK RD.

STEWARTS POINT - SKAGGS SPRINGS RD.

*These selected wineries are shown for reference. Most
offer tastings or have tours; some receive guests only
by appointment or have limited hours. Call ahead to
verify hours of operation before visiting.

STEWARTS POINT

Mendocino's dramatic coastline has made it famous all over the world, but the county offers a lot more than ocean views and rustic coastal inns. Now inland Mendocino is getting its due, thanks to local winemakers who are proving that their grapes are on a par with those of nearby Sonoma and Napa.

Vineyards were first planted here in the 1850s, when immigrants began farming food crops on the river plains and vineyards on the rugged hillsides and sun-exposed ridgetops. In time, they and their  successors found fertile ground in cooler areas that led them to achieve great success with a wide spec- trum of grape varieties. Located too far north to transport their wines to the San Francisco market by boat—as Napa and Sonoma winemakers could—Mendocino's early grape growers sold and traded their crops closer to home. In the 1960s, the wine boom and advances in shipping brought Mendocino wines to markets farther afield. Today, the county boasts eighty-four wineries, so many of them involving organic wines or vineyards that the county bills itself as "America's Greenest Wine Region."

Mendocino's pioneer spirit still flourishes and is reflected in a serious respect for the environment. Most of the county is an undeveloped, pristine landscape offering abundant opportunities for enjoying an enviable variety of outdoor pursuits.

FREY VINEYARDS, LTD.

Arguably the most low-key winery in California, this gem is hidden off a two-lane road that wends through an undeveloped corner of Redwood Valley. Unsuspecting visitors might mistake the first building for the tasting room, but that's grandma's house. They must drive past it to reach the winery, and upon arriving, they find that there is no formal tasting room. Instead, tastings are conducted over a pair of wine barrels. When everyone retires to the original fashioned from an old barn— Visitors are encouraged to picnic and benches hand-hewn by the

outdoors at a couple of planks set temperatures drop or rain falls, house—a redwood structure where the senior Mrs. Frey lives. at one of several redwood tables late family patriarch, Paul.

Virtually everything at this fashioned from something else. winery seems handmade or Barrels and tanks have been salvaged from larger operations, and the winery itself was constructed of redwood from a defunct winery in Ukiah. Some rows of grapevines are interplanted with herbs such as sage and oregano, which are harvested and distilled into aromatherapy products.

Frey (pronounced "fry") Vineyards is the oldest and largest all-organic winery in the United States. It may have another claim to fame as the winery with the most family members on the payroll. In 1961 Paul and Marguerite Frey, both doctors, bought ninety-nine acres near the headwaters of the Russian River. The Redwood Valley property seemed a great place to raise a family. Five of the couple's twelve children were born after the move, and most are still in the neighborhood.

In 1965 the Freys planted forty acres of Cabernet Sauvignon and Grey Riesling grapevines on the ranch's old pastureland, but they didn't start making wine until the 1970s. Eldest son Jonathan, who studied organic viticulture, began tending the vineyards and harvesting the grapes, which at first were sold to other wineries. When a Cabernet Sauvignon made with their grapes won a gold medal for a Santa Cruz winery, the family realized the vineyard's potential. Frey Vineyards was founded the next year, in 1980.

In 1996 the family began farming biodynamically. The word *biodynamic* stems from the agricultural theories of Austrian scientist and educator Rudolf Steiner. Biodynamic practices undertake to restore vitality to the soil. The farm is managed as a self-sustaining ecosystem, using special composting methods and specific planting times. As good stewards of the land, Frey started the first organic winery and was the first American winery fully certified by Demeter, the biodynamic certification organization. The wines have won many gold and silver medals for excellence.

FREY VINEYARDS, LTD.
14000 Tomki Rd.
Redwood Valley, CA 95470
707-485-5177
800-760-3739
info@freywine.com
www.freywine.com

OWNERS: Frey family.

LOCATION: 15 miles north of Ukiah off U.S. 101.

APPELLATION: Redwood Valley.

HOURS: By appointment.

TASTINGS: Complimentary.

TOURS: By appointment.

THE WINES: Cabernet Sauvignon, Chardonnay, Gewürztraminer, Merlot, Petite Sirah, Pinot Noir, Sangiovese, Sauvignon Blanc, Syrah, Zinfandel.

SPECIALTIES: Certified organic wines without added sulfites; biodynamically grown estate-bottled wines.

WINEMAKERS: Paul Frey, Jonathan Frey.

ANNUAL PRODUCTION: 80,000 cases.

OF SPECIAL NOTE: Picnic area for visitors' use. First American winery to receive Demeter Biodynamic® certification.

NEARBY ATTRACTIONS: Real Goods Solar Living Center (tours, store); Lake Mendocino (hiking, boating, fishing, camping); Grace Hudson Museum (Pomo Indian baskets, historical photographs, changing art exhibits); Vichy Springs (mineral springs and resort); Orr Hot Springs (mineral springs spa).

GREENWOOD RIDGE VINEYARDS

GREENWOOD RIDGE VINEYARDS
5501 Hwy. 128
Philo, CA 95466
707-895-2002
everybody@
greenwoodridge.com
www.greenwoodridge.com

OWNER: Allan Green.

LOCATION: 4 miles northwest of Philo.

APPELLATIONS: Anderson Valley, Mendocino Ridge.

HOURS: 10 A.M.–5 P.M. daily.

TASTINGS: Complimentary.

TOURS: Of the winery, by appointment.

THE WINES: Cabernet Sauvignon, Late Harvest White Riesling, Merlot, Pinot Noir, Sauvignon Blanc, Syrah, White Riesling, Zinfandel.

SPECIALTY: Home Run Red (Merlot/Zinfandel blend).

WINEMAKER: Allan Green.

ANNUAL PRODUCTION: 3,000 cases.

OF SPECIAL NOTE: A portion of Allan Green's extensive collection of wine cans, the world's largest, is on display in tasting room. Picnic area available. Winery is pet friendly. Most wines sold in Mendocino County and tasting room only.

NEARBY ATTRACTION: Hendy Woods State Park (hiking, camping).

Towering poplars shimmer behind the Greenwood Ridge Vineyards tasting room, a rough-hewn wood octagon with redwood shakes and a pointed roof. Nearby, solar panels generate the tasting room's electricity, and a sparkling pond welcomes frogs, egrets, and diving ospreys. In the center of the pond, accessed by a graceful bridge, is an island picnic area complete with redwood seating nooks. Throughout the seven-acre property, colorful pennants flutter in the breeze. Built in 1986 by winemaker Allan Green, the tasting room was designed by Green's late father, Aaron G. Green, an architect and associate of Frank Lloyd Wright. It was constructed from a single, 400-year-old redwood tree that had fallen during a storm near the family's winery and estate vineyard, located a few miles from the tasting room on Greenwood Ridge.

Perched 1,400 feet above sea level, the sixteen-acre estate vineyard is part of the Mendocino Ridge appellation, approved in 1997. Lying above the fog line and relatively close to the ocean, the appellation's vineyards grow in a sunnier climate than that found on the Anderson Valley floor. With little danger of autumn frost, grapes can remain on the vines longer and develop more complex flavors. When Green released his estate 1996 Merlot and 1997 White Riesling, they were the first wines to bear the new appellation's name. To supplement his estate fruit, Green buys Sauvignon Blanc and Zinfandel from Mendocino and Sonoma counties.

Green graduated from college with an art degree in 1971, the same year his parents bought 275 acres on Greenwood Ridge. He became a viticulturist in 1973, when the family purchased an adjoining parcel planted with Cabernet Sauvignon, Merlot, and White Riesling. To balance the effects of the cool climate and long growing season, Green adopted innovative pruning and trellising techniques. He crafted experimental lots of homemade White Riesling, seeking advice from winemakers such as Edmeades Vineyards' Jed Steele. In 1980 Green started his winery, bringing the total number of wineries in Anderson Valley at that time to four. Set near a pond beside the family's vineyards, Green's weathered winery has sharply angled rooflines and Arts and Craft–style windows. To tour the facility, visitors make an easy seven-mile drive to the top of Greenwood Ridge.

In 2001 Green redesigned his packaging in honor of his late father. It commemorates a dragon sculpture that his father gave to the Frank Lloyd Wright Foundation in 1959. Mrs. Wright had the statue engineered to breathe fire, and it remains on display at Wright's Taliesin West in Arizona. The dragon's long-tailed image curls across the winery's silk-screened labels. It serves as a fitting mascot amid the tasting room's multicolored pennants and fairytale charm.

HANDLEY CELLARS

A drive along Anderson Valley's picturesque Highway 128 reveals verdant pastures touched by sea breezes, sheep grazing behind split-rail fences, and parklike foothills meeting a clear blue sky. Among the three most westerly wineries in the valley, Handley Cellars rewards visitors with sweeping views of vineyard-stitched hills and ridgelines bristling with redwood trees. Located on the north side of the road, the low-slung winery offers relaxed tastings amid a veritable gallery of antiques and folk art. The eclectic décor includes a crocodile-shaped canoe from Papua New Guinea and elephant-themed chairs crafted ninety years ago in Thailand. The tasting bar combines a hand-carved base  from an English church with a mirrored canopy that once graced an Irish pub. Framed swatches of African Kuba cloth bear the angular patterns that inspired the winery's label art. In the adjacent courtyard garden, wisteria trails through an arbor, and picnickers can admire garden art ranging from wind chimes to Chinese dragons.

Winemaker and owner Milla Handley grew up in the Bay Area with cosmopolitan parents who made wine a regular part of the family meals. Her father, a real estate developer, owned two art galleries and traveled a great deal, collecting treasures wherever he went. A portion of his finds gives the tasting room its global flavor.

Milla Handley earned a degree in fermentation science from U.C. Davis in 1975 and three years later moved with her husband to Anderson Valley, then considered risky viticultural territory. She refined her craft working for winemakers Richard Arrowood at Chateau St. Jean and Jed Steele at Edmeades. Eager to produce wine that reflected what she deemed the "essence" of Anderson Valley, Handley began making Chardonnay in her basement. Pleased with the prize-winning results, she got serious and bought forty acres of the old Holmes Ranch. The property included a ranch house, barn, and water tower built in 1908.

Handley planted her estate vineyard in 1982, built the winery three years later, and in 1987 opened the tasting room. Behind the crush pad, she erected a solar array, which supplies 75 percent of the winery's energy. To supplement the fruit grown in her thirty-acre vineyard—certified organic in 2005—Handley planted eight more acres at her home on the ridge above the winery. She also buys grapes from vineyards throughout Mendocino County. Co-winemaker Kristen Barnhisel, who holds a master's degree in enology from U.C. Davis, joined the staff in 2004, after working at Jordan Winery and Belvedere Vineyards. Together, Handley and Barnhisel work to ensure that each wine expresses the essence of its vineyard and vintage.

HANDLEY CELLARS
3151 Hwy. 128
Philo, CA 95466
707-895-3876
800-733-3151
info@handleycellars.com
www.handleycellars.com

OWNER: Milla Handley.

LOCATION: 6 miles northwest of Philo, 15 miles from the Mendocino coast.

APPELLATIONS: Anderson Valley, Mendocino.

HOURS: 10 A.M.–6 P.M. daily in summer; 10 A.M.–5 P.M. daily in winter.

TASTINGS: Complimentary.

TOURS: By appointment.

THE WINES: Chardonnay, Gewürztraminer, Pinot Gris, Pinot Noir, Riesling, Sauvignon Blanc, Syrah, Viognier, Zinfandel.

SPECIALTIES: Estate Chardonnay, Pinot Noir, sparkling wine.

WINEMAKERS: Milla Handley, Kristen Barnhisel.

ANNUAL PRODUCTION: 12,000 cases.

OF SPECIAL NOTE: Picnic area available. Complimentary food-and-wine pairings the first weekend of each month. Art in the Cellar event held the first week of February. Locally made jewelry and international folk art and crafts for sale in tasting room. Proprietary blends, sparkling wine, and late harvest wines available in tasting room only.

NEARBY ATTRACTION: Hendy Woods State Park (hiking, camping).

JERIKO ESTATE

JERIKO ESTATE
12141 Hewlitt and
Sturtevant Rd.
Hopland, CA 95449
707-744-1140
info@jerikoestate.com
www.jerikoestate.com

OWNER: Daniel Fetzer.

LOCATION: About 2 miles
north of Hopland via
U.S. 101.

APPELLATION: Mendocino.

HOURS: 10 A.M.–5 P.M. daily.

TASTINGS: $8.50 for flights
of 6, or by the glass.

TOURS: By appointment.

THE WINES: Chardonnay,
Grenache Noir, Merlot,
Pinot Noir, Sangiovese,
Sauvignon Blanc, Syrah.

SPECIALTIES: *Méthode
champenoise* Brut and
Pinot Noir.

WINEMAKER: George Vierra.

ANNUAL PRODUCTION:
25,000 cases.

OF SPECIAL NOTE: Several
picnic sites around the
estate; gourmet food
products available in
tasting room. Annual
events include Hopland
Passport Weekend (May
and October). Brut Rosé,
Grenache Noir, and
Sauvignon Blanc available
only in tasting room.

NEARBY ATTRACTIONS:
Grace Hudson House
(museum of art, history,
and anthropology); Held-
Poage Memorial Home
and Research Library
(Mendocino County
history); Real Goods
Solar Living Center
(tours, store).

The Fetzer family has been a major force in Mendocino County winemaking for decades, ever since Barney and Kathleen Fetzer produced their first commercial wine vintage in 1968 from grapes grown on an estate they had bought ten years earlier. The family is also acclaimed for having pioneered organic grape growing in California.

Skip forward to 1997, when Daniel Fetzer, Barney and Kathleen's son, began planting Pinot Noir, Chardonnay, Syrah, Merlot, Sauvignon Blanc, and Sangiovese grapes on his own 200-acre ranch just north of Hopland. Now, vineyards that extend from the across U.S. 101 to the Russian ily heritage in another way, dynamic farming techniques. Chardonnay, in 2000, but his  he farms 120 acres of estate foothills eastward, all the way River. Staying true to his fam- Fetzer uses organic and bio- He released his first vintage, a most precious claim to fame is the distinction of having produced the county's first organic sparkling wine, a Brut, in 2001.

Fetzer decided to name his winery Jeriko Estate, evoking the ancient city of Jeriko in the region where plants and animals were first domesticated. Visitors approach the winery through a series of formidable iron gates that Fetzer embellished with crests and flanked with imposing stone columns of his own design. The view from the road offers a panoramic display of early California and Mediterranean-style architecture expressed in dun-colored, low-rise buildings topped with red tile roofs. Irregularly spaced, statuesque Canary Island date palms punctuate the Mediterranean influence. Olive trees have been planted around the visitor center. In front of the entrance, low stone walls surround a manicured field of grass divided into quadrangles in the formal Italian style. Sheep and goats can often be seen grazing around the vineyards closest to the winery, and ducks and other wildlife frequent the estate's ponds.

Behind the winemaking facility stands the original estate residence, built in 1898 by San Francisco Judge J. H. Sturtevant. Daniel Fetzer extensively redesigned the structure a century later for use as a hospitality center for VIPs. The home's color scheme provided the inspiration for the adjacent winery and visitor center, constructed in 1999. Inside the center, soaring glass walls enclose the enormous barrel room where stack after stack of aging wine is easily visible from every angle. Also on display is a casual exhibit of historic winemaking equipment, including an antique French riddling rack once used in the production of *méthode champenoise* sparkling wines.

In a corner near the tasting bar, a pair of comfortably worn leather sofas are arranged in a conversational grouping in front of a giant fireplace whose hearth extends all the way to the high ceiling.

McFADDEN VINEYARD

In 1970 Guinness McFadden planted twenty-three acres of wine grapes in Mendocino's Potter Valley. Many locals didn't think that the valley's cool, breezy climate would support quality fruit, but McFadden, a stubborn Irish New Yorker, was determined to prove them wrong. Through trial and error, he discovered that a number of varieties, including Sauvignon Blanc, Chardonnay, Pinot Gris, and Zinfandel, thrive on his farm, located about thirty-five miles north of Hopland. Over the years, McFadden has sold his fruit to esteemed wineries such as Robert Mondavi, Beringer, Sterling, and Fetzer, and delighted as they crafted it into outstanding wine. Today, McFadden cultivates 160 acres of grapes and harvests about 750 tons of fruit annually, much of which is still purchased by the region's top wineries. From the start, he has cultivated his vineyard organically, and in 1990, it received official certifica-tion from the California Certified Organic Farmers.

In Potter Valley, grapes ripen later than they do in Napa and Sonoma counties, usually well after most field workers have gone home for the winter. To ensure the availability of a picking crew, McFadden created year-round employment by planting acres of herbs, including oregano, rosemary, basil, marjoram, thyme, and lemon thyme. Ten full-time employees, whose average tenure is twenty-five years, harvest, dry, sift, and package the organically grown herbs under the McFadden Farm label. They also create garlic braids and weave California bay leaves and dried red chili peppers into holiday wreaths, many of which go to fulfill a long-term contract with Williams-Sonoma.

In 2003 McFadden launched his own label with three hundred cases of Pinot Gris. When those sold out quickly, he decided to expand his brand to include more of the varieties in his vineyard. McFadden showcases his wines in downtown Hopland in one of five bright new suites built with a raised walkway and flat facade to resemble an old western storefront. Tulip trees shade the mustard yellow and brick red building, and lamb's ear, lavender, and white roses billow below the wrought iron railing. A long, airy space with hardwood flooring and pumpkin-colored walls, the tasting room features ceramic kitchenware crafted by a local potter and items from McFadden Farm.

A raconteur fluent in five languages, including Vietnamese and Portuguese, McFadden has raised five children who now live in different parts of the country. One daughter bought a neighboring farm in Potter Valley, where she and her husband grow organic wine grapes and are introducing a third generation to the McFadden family tradition.

McFADDEN VINEYARD
Tasting Room:
13275 S. Hwy. 101, Ste. 5
Hopland, CA 95449
707-744-8463
800-544-8230
sherrilynn@
mcfaddenfarm.com
www.mcfaddenvineyard.
com

OWNER: Guinness McFadden.

LOCATION: Downtown Hopland.

APPELLATION: Potter Valley.

HOURS: 10 A.M.–5 P.M. daily.

TASTINGS: Complimentary.

TOURS: Of farm by appointment.

THE WINES: Chardonnay, Gewürztraminer, Pinot Gris, Pinot Noir, Riesling, Sauvignon Blanc, Zinfandel.

SPECIALTIES: Coro Mendocino (Zinfandel blend), sparkling wine.

WINEMAKERS: Bob Swain, Raphael Brisbois (sparkling wine).

ANNUAL PRODUCTION: 3,000 cases.

OF SPECIAL NOTE: Food-and-wine pairings by appointment. Tasting room is pet friendly. Picnic area available. Organic beef from farm sold in tasting room. Events include Hopland Passport Weekend (May and October).

NEARBY ATTRACTION: Real Goods Solar Living Center (tours, store).

MILANO FAMILY WINERY

MILANO FAMILY WINERY
14594 S. Hwy. 101
Hopland CA 95449
707-744-1396
tastingroom@
milanowinery.com
www.milanowinery.com

OWNERS: Ted and Deanna Starr.

LOCATION: .5 mile south of Hopland.

APPELLATION: Mendocino.

HOURS: 10 A.M.–5 P.M. daily.

TASTINGS: $3–$10.

TOURS: By appointment.

THE WINES: Bordeaux blends, Cabernet Sauvignon, Carignane, Charbono, Late Harvest Orange Muscat, Late Harvest Zinfandel, Malbec, Merlot, Petit Verdot, Petite Sirah, Port, Validguie, Zinfandel.

SPECIALTIES: Late-harvest wines, Ports, red wines, and sparkling wines.

WINEMAKER: Deanna Starr.

ANNUAL PRODUCTION: 3,500 cases.

OF SPECIAL NOTE: Most wines available in tasting room only. Wine-blending seminar and barbecue every June. Hopland Passport Weekend (May and October). RV parking. Tasting room sells original oil paintings and wide range of gift items.

NEARBY ATTRACTION: Real Goods Solar Living Center (tours, store).

If history has a fragrance, it probably comes close to the woodsy aroma of the old hop kiln that houses Milano Family Winery. Built in 1947 by the son-in-law of Achilles Rosetti, who operated Hopland's first winery, the structure is among the last three hop kilns in Mendocino County, and is the only one that visitors can view by appointment. From the late 1800s through the mid-1900s, local farmers grew thousands of acres of hops, whose dried flowers lend flavor to beer. The aptly named town of Hopland, less than a mile north of the winery, underscores the former dominance of the crop.

In 2001 Deanna and Ted Starr acquired the property—which first produced wine in 1977 and is the oldest working winery in Hopland—and restored its original name, Milano. The couple came from Southern California, where Deanna had worked for more than twenty years as a registered nurse and manager in the medical field. With her background in chemistry, she felt confident that she could translate the couple's passion for wine into a vinicultural career. Ted, who designed software for medical applications, had developed a successful program to help winery owners manage their business, and was equally eager for a more rural way of life.

Set at the foot of Duncan's Peak, well back from a quiet stretch of Highway 101, the seven-acre parcel resembles a tidy farm, complete with a menagerie of animals. Jacob's sheep graze in a green pasture, roosters wander freely, and ducks flutter near a creek bed. There are pygmy goats, land tortoises, Sebastopol curly feathered geese, a llama, a pot-bellied pig named Willy, and two Labrador retrievers, Cuvee and Merlot.

Stepping up to the second-floor tasting room—where hops once cured on redwood slats—visitors can see the clear grain of the now-rare heart redwood from which the three-story structure was built. Tastings take place at a chest-high bar, and windows afford views of neighboring vineyards growing opposite the highway. A winemaker, but admittedly not a farmer, Deanna procures her fruit from a handful of dedicated growers, most of them in Mendocino County. The winery is certified organic and does produce a few organic wines among a wide variety of big reds and quirky whites.

Visitors to Milano Family Winery who schedule a tour will likely find Deanna leading it, sharing her story with enthusiasm. She often stops to offer samples in the cool barrel room downstairs, where workers once bundled dried hops.

Acknowledgments

Creativity, perseverance, integrity, and commitment are fundamental qualities
for guaranteeing the success of a project. The artistic and editorial teams who worked on
this edition possess these qualities in large measures. My heartfelt thanks go to K. Reka Badger
and Marty Olmstead, writers; Robert Holmes, photographer; Judith Dunham, copyeditor;
Linda Bouchard, proofreader; Poulson Gluck Design, production; and Ben Pease, cartographer.

In addition, I am grateful for the invaluable counsel and encouragement of Chester and
Frances Arnold; Greg Taylor; my esteemed parents — Estelle Silberkleit and William Silberkleit;
Danny Biederman; and the scores of readers and winery enthusiasts who have contacted me
to say how much they enjoy this book series.

I also extend my deepest appreciation to Keo Hornbostel of the Hyatt Vineyard Creek
Hotel & Spa in Santa Rosa; Todd Iseri of the Napa Valley Marriott Hotel & Spa in
the city of Napa; Jeff Perry and Alexis Swan of the Best Western Sonoma Valley Inn
in the town of Sonoma; and Sarah Noguera of the Hampton Inn in Ukiah
for their superb hospitality and enthusiastic support of this project.

And finally, for her love and creative input, as well as for enduring work-filled weekends
and midnight deadlines, my gratitude and affection go to Lisa Silberkleit.

— Tom Silberkleit

OTHER BOOKS BY WINE HOUSE PRESS

The California Directory of Fine Wineries — Central Coast
Santa Barbara • San Luis Obispo • Paso Robles

Wine House Press
127 East Napa Street, Suite F, Sonoma, CA 95476
707-996-1741

Editor and publisher: Tom Silberkleit
Original design: Jennifer Barry Design
Production: Poulson Gluck Design
Copy editor: Judith Dunham
Cartographer: Ben Pease
Artistic development: Lisa Silberkleit
Proofreader: Linda Bouchard

All photographs by Robert Holmes, except the following: page 19, bottom right: courtesy Beaulieu Vineyards;
page 39, bottom right: Lisa Sze; page 48, bottom left: courtesy Kuleto Estate; page 71: courtesy Terlato Family;
page 74: creativedirections.com; page 79, middle, courtesy Spring Mountain Vineyard; page 122,
bottom right: Stan Esecson; page 125, bottom left: Mary Rogers; page 150: Jamey Thomas.

Front cover photograph: Kuleto Estate, Napa Valley, CA
Back cover photographs: top left: Mumm Napa; top right: Robert Mondavi Winery;
bottom left: Hartford Family Winery; bottom right: Beringer Vineyards.

Printed and bound in Singapore through DNP America, LLC
ISBN-13: 978-0-9724993-5-4

Fifth Edition

Distributed by Publishers Group West, 1700 Fourth Street, Berkeley, CA 94710, www.pgw.com

The publisher has made every effort to ensure the accuracy of the information contained in
The California Directory of Fine Wineries, but can accept no liability for any loss, injury, or inconvenience
sustained by any visitor as a result of any information or recommendation contained in this guide.
Travelers should always call ahead to confirm hours of operation, fees, and other highly variable information.

Always act responsibly when drinking alcoholic beverages by selecting a designated driver or prearranged transportation.

Customized Editions
Wine House Press will print custom editions of this volume for bulk purchase at your request. Personalized covers
and foil-stamped corporate logo imprints can be created in large quantities for special promotions or events, or as premiums.
For more information, contact Custom Imprints, Wine House Press, 127 E. Napa Street, Suite F, Sonoma, CA 95476; 707-996-1741.

www.CaliforniaFineWineries.com

Join the Facebook Fan Page:
www.facebook.com/pages/California-Directory-of-Fine-Wineries/106071659444130

Follow us on Twitter:
twitter.com/cafinewineries